YOU CAN'T MARRY
YOUR MOTHER~IN~LAW
AND OTHER COMMON
LEGAL MISCONCEPTIONS

You Can't Marry Your Mother-in-Law
by Maureen Mullally

© 2006 Lawpack Publishing Limited

Cartoons © 2006 Rupert Besley

Lawpack Publishing Limited
76–89 Alscot Road
London SE1 3AW

www.lawpack.co.uk

All rights reserved.
Printed in Great Britain

ISBN-10: 1-905261-28-4
ISBN-13: 978-1-905261-28-4

Exclusion of Liability and Disclaimer

YOU CAN'T MARRY YOUR MOTHER~IN~LAW

AND OTHER COMMON LEGAL MISCONCEPTIONS

∽ Maureen Mullally ∾

CONTENTS

ABOUT THE AUTHOR

Maureen Mullally read law at King's College, University of London. She was called to the Bar at Gray's Inn. She is also a member of Middle Temple where, from her Chambers in Lamb Building, she practised family law for 27 years. During that period she was called to the Irish Bar at King's Inns in Dublin.

Maureen has written several books, setting out the law relating to the family in England and Wales, and in Ireland, in simple language. For the past five years she has contributed a weekly column on topics relating to law and the family in the Universe newspaper.

She has broadcast many radio interviews on aspects of family law, and contributed to many publications, including *Family Law Journal*, *The Times*, *Good Housekeeping* and the *Daily Mail*.

Maureen now practises as a mediator at the South East London Family Mediation Bureau, helping separating couples to reach their own agreements about children, finance and property, rather than go through the trauma and expense of court battles. She is a Member of the UK College of Family Mediators.

Maureen has seven children and thirteen grandchildren who keep her occupied in her spare time. She plays golf and bridge, and enjoys the theatre and music.

INTRODUCTION

Lawpack publish an official disclaimer, but I would just like to add my personal and most sincere apology to any real lawyer who perceives that I have got something in his or her area of expertise hopelessly wrong.

These little vignettes are an expression of my own individual and lighthearted approach to a number of dearly cherished misconceptions about various quirky aspects of the law of England and Wales. They are intended not for instruction but for diversion; hopefully, every reader will find something to amuse or surprise.

A venerable instructing solicitor of mine was in the habit of ringing me up at home at the most inconvenient moments – a favourite time was 8 o'clock on a Sunday morning, when my long-suffering husband would correctly predict 'That can only be Hymie.'

As it invariably was. Hymie would preface the conversation with the words 'Just wanted to ask you for some advice under section 1 [2] [b] of the Old Pals Act.'

I have shamelessly invoked that very section in plaguing colleagues and friends at my Chambers in Lamb Building for advice and guidance in the preparation of this book. They have been more than patient and kind. I am enormously grateful to them. I have also had limitless support and encouragement from all the members of my family, some of whom are lawyers and some of whom understand the mysteries of my computer, impenetrable as far as I am concerned.

So this book is dedicated to all of them – they must be so glad to hear that it is finished at last! I hasten to reiterate that any howlers are my sole responsibility.

Maureen Mullally

A NEW RELATIONSHIP WITH YOUR MOTHER-IN-LAW

This may come as a surprise, but it's now legally permissible to marry your mother-in-law or, for that matter, your son-in-law, daughter-in-law or father-in-law. While this news is not very likely to generate countrywide queues at register offices, it does represent a substantial revolution in the law relating to just who you can – and who you can't – marry.

The ruling was made by the European Court of Human Rights in an English case where a father-in-law (let's call him F) and his daughter-in-law (let's call her D) fell in love with one another. Whether D was at the relevant time still married to F's son, or F still married to D's mother-in-law, or both, is unclear.

Confused? You may want to sketch out a family tree on a spare bit of paper!

Be that as it may, by the time F and D applied to a register office in the hope of formalising their union, both had been divorced, so were technically free to marry. The snag was that one, or both, of their original spouses, F's son or D's mother-in-law, was still alive. Had

this been otherwise, and both F and D were over the age of 21 – which seems likely – an exception to the general rule could have been granted.

The Registrar to whom the application was made consulted the Marriage (Prohibited Degrees of Relationship) Act of 1986 and, in the light of the fact that the circumstances were not those in which the exception could operate, refused to perform the ceremony.

Undaunted, F and D sought legal advice. The law is exceedingly slow and cumbersome, as anyone who has been unfortunate enough to be involved with it will be only too aware. By the time the case wound its way through the English courts and eventually got to the European Court, F and D had been an item for nine years and had a child.

But their child was not the only infant involved in this complex story. Another had been born to D and F's son-in-law during their marriage. Do you want to go back to the diagram? To tease out this child's legal relationship with the various personalities in this tangled tale will strain the competence of the most expert delineator of family trees.

For starters, on the marriage of F and D, this child, already the grandchild of F, would take on an additional role as his step-child, and D would become the step-grandmother of her own child! Her second child would become his half-brother, while simultaneously being transformed into his uncle. I need hardly go on.

Article 12 of the Convention on Human Rights, now incorporated into English law, protects the right to marry and to found a family. The judges considered that, in real life, situations like this are bound to arise; fathers-in-law will fall in love with their daughters-in-law and that love will be reciprocated.

In a nutshell, they came to the view that the refusal to marry F and D was a breach of their fundamental human rights under Article 12.

Will this spell the death knell for all those mother-in-law jokes?

∾ MISCEPTION # TWO ∾

DEFENDING THE GUILTY

Ask any barrister. That's exactly what non-lawyers do. From the moment they discover your occupation at any social gathering, they make a point of cornering you, beady-eyed with suspicion, 'There's something I've always wondered…' Your heart sinks. You know precisely what the next sentence will be: 'I've always wanted to understand how you can defend someone you know to be guilty.'

You may be a corporate law whiz, you may be an intellectual property star, you may touch nothing outside family law – none of that matters in the slightest to your new acquaintance. If you are a barrister, a major part of your job is assumed to be the defence of guilty criminals. And a pretty discreditable part of your job it is, in his or her opinion.

You try to suppress a sigh as you struggle to give a satisfactory account of yourself. You explain that your expertise doesn't happen to lie in the criminal jurisdiction. However, you have been trained in your youth, as have all practitioners at the Bar, how you should approach the defence of criminals, whether guilty or otherwise.

Members of the general public are usually quite astounded to be told that you do not ask your clients whether they are guilty or not. You merely take their instructions as to how they wish to plead to the offences with which they have been charged. Your job is then to present their version of events before the court and the jury, if there is one, as persuasively as you can.

'But hang on a minute,' your interrogator will protest, 'you must know when your client is obviously guilty.'

'Know' in this context is a curious word. You may be virtually certain of someone's guilt – it may be as plain as the nose on your questioner's face. Happily, however, it is not your job to determine guilt or innocence. This task falls to the tribunal or, in graver cases, to the 12 citizens charged with that responsibility.

This, however, isn't likely to satisfy your pursuer. 'Ah,' the person will proclaim triumphantly, 'but what if the criminal admits it to you?'

Most criminals are, in fact, completely au fait with the rules; those who are not will have had them explained by their associates. Consequently, they wouldn't dream of admitting any such thing to their defending counsel.

So it would be a rarity for a barrister to be taken into a client's confidence to the extent of an admission. In that unlikely event, it has to be explained that there are now only two choices for the accused: one is to plead guilty and allow the barrister to mitigate – in other words, to offer an excuse or draw attention to circumstances which may, with luck, attract a lesser sentence. The other choice is to find a new barrister, who will not be told the truth.

Your pursuer will probably look unconvinced. As a member of the Bar, I wish I'd been able to extract a fee for every time I've had to suffer this conversation.

AS A PARENT, I MUST BE CONSULTED

As a parent, you have the right to be consulted about any decision which is going to affect your child – correct? Well, up to a point. You will certainly be consulted if your child needs medical attention at school, depending on what that medical attention is.

Most schools will ensure that parents are informed if, for example, their child falls down in the playground and a sticking plaster has to be applied, or if an aspirin is to be administered for a headache.

However, you may not be consulted about the sex education given at the school. Some primary schools are now explaining methods of contraception and abortion to children whose parents may think that they are too young to understand these matters. And, when it comes to a teenager who is found to be pregnant, it has recently become clear that a school is legally entitled to withhold that information from the girl's parents. Your young daughter can have an appointment made for her at an abortion clinic by a school teacher, who will sometimes accompany her there to have the operation performed.

At a time when you would think that a daughter would need her mother most, schools have claimed that the 1988 Data Protection Act gives a pregnant teenager an absolute right to confidentiality. Even if the school authorities would have wanted the parents to be informed, it appears that they must preserve that confidentiality.

What happens when the child needs post-operative care can only be surmised. At the very least, you would think that she needs the love and support of her family at this crisis point in her life. How can her parents provide it if they have no idea about the situation she is in?

Similarly, parents can be kept in the dark when their child is to appear in court, charged with a criminal offence. Yet at the same time they are held responsible and can be sentenced to prison for offences which their children might commit: truanting, for example, or breaking Anti-Social Behaviour Orders.

'Parental rights' are a bit of a joke today. Parents have a multitude of responsibilities heaped upon them by the law, but the idea that they should expect the corresponding rights, which have been taken for granted by previous generations, has now become laughable. Conversely, children are given rights with apparently no responsibilities attached to them.

The nanny state is taking over the traditional role of the parent. Professionals such as child carers, teachers, doctors and lawyers are considered to be much better at carrying out decision making in the interests of our children than those whose only qualifications are that they are mothers and fathers.

Never mind – you can still decide important matters like what clothing they should wear, how their hair should be cut, and what time they should go to bed. That is, of course, if they will let you.

∽ MISCONCEPTION # FOUR ∾

THAT SHOP HAS TO SELL ME THAT SWEATER AT THE MARKED PRICE

You catch sight of it in the shop window. Just the garment you had been looking for. Incredibly, the price tag is much lower than you would have expected. You check the quality of the material. Very impressive. This is a real bargain. The assistant confirms that they have it in your size.

Yes, you'll have it. If you hesitate, someone else may beat you to the purchase. Out comes your wallet and you offer the sum marked on the ticket in the window. The assistant gasps. She tells you that there's been a mistake. A nought has been missed out. The cost of the garment is in fact ten times what you had been led to believe.

What is your legal position? Many people think that in this situation the shop is legally obliged to sell you the item at the marked price, even though there may have been a genuine mistake. Unfortunately, here you will discover yourself to be mired in the intricacies of the law of contract.

Any exchange between a buyer and a seller is legally termed a contract. To establish that there has been a

contract, it has to be shown that there has been an offer and an acceptance. Hang on, you say; this is exactly what has happened here, isn't it? The seller made an offer on the price tag in the window and I accepted it. So I have the right to buy it at that offered price.

Sadly for you, the law of contract, in its ineffable wisdom, does not take this view, even though most right-minded people might consider it to be the obvious one. The ticketed price is known, in contract law, as 'an invitation to treat'. The word 'treat' here carries the old-fashioned meaning of 'negotiate'. You have accepted the invitation to treat by making the offer to buy. It's then open to the shop to accept your offer or not, so there is no contract until the salesperson has accepted your offer.

The reverse case is exemplified in many foreign markets where, as a matter of course, the vendor, when asked the price of an item, will start the bidding at a sum which may be ten times what he or she actually expects you to give him. The subsequent hard bargaining is all part of the excitement of shopping in exotic locations.

Perhaps you might get a bargain in the sweater after all. Many shops, for the sake of their reputation, might be prepared to come down on the real asking price in order to make a sale and in acknowledgement that the mistake has been theirs. But don't expect to get a 90 per cent reduction. For that you would really need to find yourself in a souk.

I'M BRITISH – I HAVE A RIGHT TO BE TRIED HERE

If you're a British citizen and it's alleged that you have committed a crime here, you have a right to be tried in the British courts. Right? Wrong, unfortunately for you, if the crime you are alleged to have committed attracts the attention of the United States.

It must have seemed like a good idea at the time. Our government and the American government took the view that, in the ongoing war against terrorism, it would be helpful if suspects could be extradited from one country to another without the time-consuming process of formal investigation into their cases in the country acceding to the extradition.

In 2003 Parliament enacted the appropriate legislation, giving the US the right to insist on the extradition of individuals the Americans wished to have tried in their courts. But the law of unforeseen consequences has come into operation, as it so often seems to do when the government has a good idea and rushes to enshrine it in legislation without giving it any proper consideration.

Incredibly, the first of these unanticipated consequences has been the adamant refusal of Congress to enact reciprocal legislation in our favour. It is rumoured that the Irish-American lobby are anxious to ensure that those suspected of terrorist offences related to the Northern Irish conflict should not be extradited to this country.

Another result, which ought to have been predictable if real thought had been given to the drafting of the Bill, is that the right given to the Americans is not confined to cases where terrorism is suspected.

The result is that we have an 'Alice-in-Wonderland' situation where our authorities have complied with requests from the US, in the absence of any vestige of mutual benefit to us. The most celebrated instance, so far, has been that of the 'NatWest three'. It has been alleged that these three employees of the NatWest Bank in London made illegal financial gains in the course of their employment. The interest of the American government in their case stems from its association with other alleged crimes committed in relation to the Enron organisation.

The crimes, if such they were, were committed here. The loser – NatWest – is here. All the potential witnesses are here. But Charles Clarke, then Home Secretary, ruled that the request for their extradition must be complied with. A High Court Judge, no doubt reluctantly, confirmed that there was no way around the law. An appeal to the House of Lords was unsuccessful, as was an application to the European Court of Human Rights.

So the three accused have been extradited and will probably face at least a pre-trial year in the US, separated from their families and friends. To defend themselves, they will have to pay the travel costs for their English lawyers and numerous witnesses. Even if they are found innocent, it seems that they will be unable to recover their costs, estimated to be $1.5 to $2 million each.

We can't demand the extradition of any American citizen to be tried here. You couldn't make it up, could you?

SOBER AS A JUDGE...?

Well, judges are as human as the rest of us, despite their rather forbidding appearance on the Bench. Most of them, in my experience, enjoy a decent glass of wine or two when off-duty. Do they never overindulge?

Certainly, it is within my knowledge that at least one eminent appeal judge of the past, who shall be nameless for obvious reasons, had to plead guilty to a drink driving charge resulting from a too convivial evening at a Middle Temple dinner.

Ought he to have resigned? Been removed? A pragmatic approach was taken. He remained in post, but the listing officer made sure that he never sat on appeals in relation to offences where alcohol had been a constituent element.

Judicial noddings off during the weary afternoon sessions in actual trials are not completely unknown – whether drink related or not. It only happened to me on one occasion: I glanced up in the middle of my most compelling submission to realise that my tribunal had fallen into a gentle doze. What to do? Exhibiting great presence of mind, I deliberately elbowed a weighty tome of legal precedents to the floor with an almighty clatter, to be rewarded by a start as my judge returned to consciousness!

Of course, it is counsel's duty to use his or her best endeavours not to be so boring in an exposition of legal argument that the judge's mind is tempted to wander. A friend of mine had been appearing in the Court of Appeal and later that day, at a social function, met one of the judges before whom his case had been heard.

And further may I venture herewith to contend...

Enthusiastically my friend reminded the learned judge that he had been appearing before him that very afternoon. 'Yes, indeed,' was the courteous reply. 'And I have to tell you that, as I listened to your submissions, I began to lose the will to live.'

Fictional judges who appear in some television series tend to behave in ways which would never be tolerated in real life. The powers-that-be take great trouble to ensure that any candidate for a judicial post is suitable in every way. Interviewed by the Lord Chancellor's Department for a minor role in the courts, I was taken aback by the final question from my interrogator, 'Is there anything in your life which might embarrass the Lord Chancellor?'

Put to you like that, you tend to feel guilty immediately, however blameless your life may be. How easily embarrassed is the Lord Chancellor, you wonder. Frantically, you make a mental trawl of your habits and pursuits before you find that your voice is faltering an unconvincing denial of anything remotely improper about your existence.

All that having been said, it's my sincere belief that we are lucky enough to have an impressively competent and hardworking body of men and women presiding over our courts. It is no harm to bear in mind that they are human too.

IN ENGLAND AND WALES WE HAVE 'NO FAULT' DIVORCE

Well, we do – or we did – or did we? The plans were elaborately laid and well meant. The powers-that-be had come to the conclusion that the only thing wrong with divorce was the unfortunate tendency for divorcing couples to become bitter, antagonistic and vengeful over the existing grounds for obtaining a decree.

There were – still are – five: adultery, unreasonable behaviour, two years of desertion, two years of separation with consent to the divorce, and five years of separation without consent.

Civilised and patient couples will wait until they have been separated for two years and will then agree to divorce. Nothing hurtful need be alleged against anyone. But two years is a long time. And, however bad their marriages may have been, it is astounding how many contemplating a divorce are anxious to get it over as quickly as possible so they can rush into marriage with someone else. You could call it a triumph of hope over experience.

There are two quick ways to achieve a decree: you can allege and prove that your spouse has committed adultery or you can allege and satisfy the court that he or she has behaved so unreasonably that no reasonable person could be expected to live with him or her.

Adultery is bad enough. But for real fall-out just consider 'unreasonable behaviour'. The sad fact is that any competent family lawyer can construct an unreasonable behaviour petition from the basic day-to-day to and fro of any marriage. But just wait until the recipient of that petition reads what has been alleged about him or her! For the sake of a speedy process, pride and bile may be swallowed, but the allegations will rankle and fester poisoning subsequent negotiations about children, money and property, usually and unfortunately to the considerable detriment of the children.

It was decided that it was in the best interests of everyone concerned that these five ways of concluding a marriage should be thrown out, to be replaced by the entirely neutral ground that the marriage had irretrievably broken down.

Couples planning to divorce would attend seminars explaining the process and how to resolve all issues amicably. You could petition after only a year of marriage. Decrees would be granted in no time at all and without inter-spousal warfare. It all seemed sensible enough.

The law was actually passed. But it has never been put into effect – just quietly shelved. The trouble seems to have been the financial and logistic practicalities. It was all going to cost a lot more than had been thought. So, after the expenditure of a great deal of Parliamentary time and taxpayers' money, we are back where we were.

And divorce still generates bitterness, acrimony and vengeful feelings. Maybe this would still have been the case even if we had taken the 'no fault' route. Apparently, we will never know.

How informative are Home Information Packs?

The plan is that Home Information Packs (HIPs) are to be compulsory from 1 June 2007. From that date, no-one will be able to buy or sell a home in England or Wales without a compulsory pack.

These packs, the brainchild of John Prescott when he had oversight of property matters, were claimed to be the answer to all the problems traditionally associated with buying a house; 'gazumping', for example, where a better offer is accepted by the vendor before there has been an exchange of contracts. This can be incredibly frustrating and expensive to a hopeful purchaser who has made an offer and has already incurred solicitors' and surveyors' fees, confident that it has been accepted.

Another inconvenience which, it is said, would have been ameliorated by the packs, is the 'chain' – where several transactions depend on other deals, which may or may not break down, leaving everyone concerned gibbering with fury and out of pocket into the bargain. Currently, over a quarter of all property transactions fail between the acceptance of an offer and the exchange of legally binding contracts. Surveys and searches can only be set in motion once an offer has been accepted. But nobody is under a legal obligation to stick to the price agreed until contracts are exchanged, and that doesn't happen until all the legal niceties have been sorted.

HIPs were to contain the results of searches plus a 'home condition report', prepared by an 'inspector'. The qualifications for inspectors were left unspecified – what very soon became clear was that they were being recruited and trained in insufficient numbers to cope with the predicted demand for their services.

In July 2006, less than a year before the launch date, the government climbed down and announced that the packs would not have to contain the home condition report, but that the scheme would be 'phased in'. Whether the limited packs will still be compulsory is not entirely clear.

It was to have been the responsibility of the seller, rather than the purchaser, to meet the cost of collating the information for the pack. Professionals were forecasting that the packs would cost £1,000. Prospective suppliers of the limited packs are predicting that even these will cost around £800.

So what happens if the packs are out of date? Might they be open to fraud or misrepresentation by dishonest sellers? 'Caveat emptor', explains the government website, 'will apply'. Disregarding the little difficulty that few prospective purchasers will be Latin scholars, what this means in plain English is that the buyer's conveyancer will be responsible for checking the documents in the pack for accuracy – in other words, both seller and buyer will be paying.

It remains to be seen whether the 'phasing in' will start on time. One thing is sure, however: HIPS are going to mean more expense for everyone.

IT'S A DOG'S LIFE

This expression has never been used to imply that a dog's life is anything to be envied. But the government is all set to change that, with legislation which will amount to a bill of 'human' rights for domestic pets.

Whether it is justifiable to spend parliamentary time and energy on ensuring a comfortable existence for dogs, cats, canaries and tortoises in these troubled times of war, famine and global warming is a question which many of us will be asking ourselves. Possibly the measure is seen as a vote winner – we think a lot of our pets in this country. Some children may be living in poverty due to our inability to organise an efficient child support agency. Others may be enduring sexual or emotional abuse due to shortages of competent social workers. But it's the idea that an animal may be suffering which seems to get most of us really upset. You only have to compare the Royal Society for the Prevention of Cruelty to Animals (RSPCA) with the National Society for the Prevention of Cruelty to Children (NSPCC) – no royal patronage – to discover where our priorities lie.

So it should come as no surprise to learn that Margaret Beckett, prior to her appointment as Foreign

Secretary, was spending time, as the Environment Secretary, drafting leaflets to be issued to all pet owners, describing in the case of each species, precisely how the animal should be cared for.

Pets will have five statutory freedoms under the new legislation. The codes of conduct for owners set out regulations for correct feeding, toilet arrangements and the provision of 'mental stimulation'. Each code, it's anticipated, will run into many pages, and will form part of the Animal Welfare Act, when it comes into force.

The word is that the first code to be drafted relates to cats. Cats must be kept indoors at night, for their own protection and that of local wildlife. Cats will have to be neutered at four months, because cats can produce up to 18 kittens a year and, as the code points out, 'motherhood takes a lot out of cats'.

Owners will be expected to provide areas where their cats can find hiding places, such as an enclosed bed or box, together with a high shelf or ledge where the cat can escape from nuisances like children and other pets. Cats must be mentally stimulated to prevent them from becoming bored or frustrated. In a section devoted to going to the toilet, it's laid down that owners must ensure their cats have privacy, by giving them a 'hidden away' place to relieve themselves. Another guideline sets out that cats should be introduced to dogs 'very

carefully'. Any owner of a cat or a dog could already have told Margaret Beckett that.

What has not yet been explained is the method by which your pet will issue a complaint that his or her owner is in breach of the code, nor do we know to whom the complaint should be issued. Yet we already have legislation to protect animals from cruelty. Giving them a bill of rights looks like another waste of parliamentary time and taxpayers' money.

TRESPASSERS WON'T BE PROSECUTED

'Trespassers will be prosecuted'. This stern admonition may not be as popular as it once was, but most of us will remember coming across these words warning uninvited visitors that they could be leaving themselves open to retribution imposed with the weight of the full majesty of the law behind it. The notices might be attached to the walls of premises, or on signposts erected at the boundaries of private properties. You can still find examples, on occasion, to this day.

Whether or not they succeed in intimidating anyone intent on entering is a matter of speculation. The truth is that, from a legal point of view, they are quite meaningless; lawyers are in the habit of dismissing the notice, somewhat derisively, as 'the wooden lie'.

Why? Does this mean that the owner of land or property has no legal redress against unwanted intruders? Not at all, in fact. But trespass is not a criminal offence for which the guilty party can be prosecuted in the criminal courts. He or she can only be sued for his or her misbehaviour in the civil courts. Possibly trespassers will be sued' just does not quite have the same menacing ring to it.

Non-lawyers can be confused – understandably so! – by the fact that there are not one, but two separate and distinct legal systems in this country – the civil and the criminal. In the civil courts you can be sued by a plaintiff;

in the criminal you can be prosecuted in the name of the Crown. In both, however, you will be called the 'defendant'.

So does this mean that there are two completely separate court systems? Well, yes and no. There are criminal courts and there are civil courts, certainly. But it's not just as simple as that. Some lower courts, Magistrates' Courts in particular, deal with both civil and criminal cases. The most serious cases will then go to specialised courts. In the event of an appeal from one of these, the appeal will be heard in the Court of Appeal, which hears both types of case, as does the House of Lords – the final arbiter in our system. Unless, that is, an aggrieved party decides to take the matter to the European Court.

Criminal courts can, and do, impose sentences of imprisonment in appropriate circumstances. Civil remedies are likely to take the form of damages – financial recompense for any loss sustained. However, judges hearing civil cases also have the power, in certain circumstances, to impose custodial sentences. No wonder you need a lawyer to disentangle it all!

And what do you do if you want to threaten potential intruders and you don't feel that 'Trespassers will be sued' packs much of a punch? I suppose you could always fall back on that other time-honoured battle cry, 'See you in court!'

I WANT CUSTODY OF MY CHILD

Somehow, you can't help feeling that Solomon may have had a point. Two women came before him, each claiming to be the mother of a particular baby. In those far off pre-DNA days, you would have thought that no judge could solve such a dilemma. But Solomon isn't famed for his wisdom for nothing. Having listened carefully to each of the women, he handed down his judgment. Since it was impossible for him to determine who was the real mother, he ordered that the baby be cut in two, half to be given to each. That quickly solved the riddle. The real mother was prepared to let the other woman have her child, rather than let it be slaughtered.

People still fight over children, but nowadays these battles take place when the parents separate. The breakdown of any relationship generates feelings of grief, failure, anger and bitterness. When the couple have children, all too often those children unwittingly take on the role of handy weapons in an ongoing conflict. The parents are so wrapped up in their own feelings that they cannot see the damage that they are doing to their children. Bewildered and hurt, the children frequently try to please both parents, the two most important

people in the world to them. All too often the sad culmination takes the form of a pitched and expensive battle in a court of law.

Newspapers, magazines, television and radio programmes all cling tenaciously to the idea that a parent can get 'custody' of his or her child in divorce proceedings. They also insist on talking about 'access' – in other words, visiting rights – to children. As a result, it is hardly surprising that most people believe that such things as custody and access orders are still in existence, when in fact the concepts of 'custody' and 'access' were abolished many years ago by Parliament. The words are old fashioned and carry false implications that the person with whom the child lives has custody – in other words, 'owns' the child – whereas the non-resident parent can be granted 'access', as it were, as a favour.

When the courts have to make orders now, they are described as 'residence' and 'contact' orders. Until the passage of the Children Act in 1989, the courts always had to make orders about any children involved in families where the parents were divorcing. This was the case even when two perfectly sensible parents had taken the trouble to work out between them what would be the best arrangements for the children after their separation. Now, however, the court only makes orders about children when the parents are incapable of coming to an agreement. This emphasises that it's the parents who have the primary responsibility for deciding what will be in the best interests of their own children.

The change in terminology was in the – vain, as it turns out – hope that 'residence' and 'contact' would prove less inflammatory. Unfortunately, some couples still insist on perpetuating the warfare between them in arguments about the children. Bring back Solomon, do I hear you cry?

୬ MISCONCEPTION # TWELVE ୭

FORBIDDEN FRUIT

What can you do about those overhanging branches when your neighbour allows them to encroach upon your garden? You can, of course, politely request him or her to cut them back, so that your lawn and flowerbeds, of which you happen to be justly proud after all the hours of hard work you spend on them, resume their usual manicured and orderly appearance.

But some neighbours just aren't terribly neighbourly. Polite requests can fall on deaf ears. There are people who are not all that bothered about how their own gardens look, let alone yours. So can you take matters into your own hands and do a bit of pruning yourself, even though the actual trees, shrubs or bushes are firmly rooted in your neighbour's plot and, consequently, clearly belong there?

It is, in fact, long-established law that you are permitted to do this. You must, however, take care to confine your pruning to vegetation which strays over your own boundary.

When you have carried out this energetic task and a satisfactory pile of branches results on your side of the

Been some year for plums, eh!

fence, you may be tempted to think of making a bonfire of it, or possibly chopping it up to use indoors as firewood. On no account should you yield to either temptation. In law, the cut branches still belong to your neighbour. Ideally, how they are to be disposed of should be the subject of an amicable discussion between you, but by this time your relationship may have deteriorated to the point where you need the advice of a friendly local solicitor.

Just suppose the overhanging branches are fruit bearing. Surely you can help yourself to apples, pears or plums actually ripening over your property? The legal answer is that you can't. The fruit still belongs to your neighbour. If, by this time, you are not on speaking terms, exactly how the neighbour is to access your property, in order to collect his or her fruit, the law does not make clear. So the fruit, ungathered and overripe, eventually falls to the ground. Your ground. At this point it must have become yours, mustn't it? You could at least collect a few windfalls, bottle them, freeze them or make them into jam, couldn't you?

It is almost 100 years since judges of the King's Bench Division, hearing an appeal from Maidstone County Court, upheld the decision of that court in a case followed to this day. The defendant had picked apples from branches of a neighbour's tree, which overhung his garden, and sold them. He lost the case. The court found in favour of the plaintiff, the owner of the tree.

So be careful about what fruit you pick. An admonition which dates back to Adam and Eve, you may recall.

I DON'T NEED TO MAKE A WILL

It is surprising how many of us don't feel the need to make a will and this can apply to lawyers, who ought to know better. We are not keen on being reminded of our own mortality, of course, and many of us put a will on the long finger, believing that there will be plenty of time to make one when we are older. The unpleasant reality is that there may not be.

Others of us, if we think about wills at all, have some vague idea that it isn't important to make one. After all, when we die, those we love will automatically inherit everything we have, won't they?

People who think this way would be astonished and upset to be confronted with the facts. In the first place, if you die intestate – without having made a will – the taxman will help himself to a hefty slice of your financial assets, considerably more than would be the case had a will existed.

Even worse, your assets may be divided in a way which would be totally against your wishes and intentions. There is a strict legal hierarchy laid down when it comes to inheritance under intestacy – and it.

may include the last people in the world whom you would wish to derive any benefit from your estate. For example, most people survived by a husband or wife would expect that he or she would simply inherit everything. The fact is that if the couple have children, the widowed spouse will get the chattels (i.e. furniture and bits and pieces), plus the sum of £125,000. Don't forget that if you own a house, your estate is likely to be worth a lot more than that.

So what happens to the rest of it? The surviving spouse gets only the interest on one half of the remainder for life, after the £125,000 has been deducted. The children share the other half of the remainder immediately, but must wait for the death of the surviving parent before getting the half in which he or she had a life interest.

If you have no children or grandchildren, but your parents are still alive, your spouse would get the first £200,000 and half the remainder. Your parents get the other half. If your parents are deceased but you have brothers and sisters, those brothers and sisters will share the other half of the remainder.

If you are cohabiting with your partner, rather than being married or in a registered gay partnership, he or she simply doesn't enter into the picture. Partners get nothing, while relatives for whom you may have little or no time can scoop the lot.

I could go on, but you probably have enough information now to realise that making a will is a very good idea indeed, so make it a priority!

AN ENGLISHMAN'S HOME
IS HIS CASTLE

One of our most treasured beliefs has been that our homes are our own space. Unless it is alleged that we have been guilty of some crime or misdemeanour, and a search warrant has been obtained, no-one has the right to enter our property uninvited. As law-abiding citizens, we are free to live our lives in total privacy behind our closed front doors.

Not, however, if an idea of John Prescott's takes hold. In pursuit of the re-rating plans for council tax, now postponed until after the local elections, he proposed that local councils should be able to appoint inspectors. These officials would be empowered to turn up unannounced on people's doorsteps and demand entry into their homes. Anyone who refused admission to one of these inspectors would be liable to a fine of £500, and end up with a criminal record into the bargain.

The purpose of the visit would be to establish whether, in the opinion of the inspector, the occupier of the property had enhanced its value in some way – by installing a fitted kitchen, for example, or a new shower

unit. The addition of a conservatory or the landscaping of a garden would probably also be considered a 'value-significant feature, to be solemnly recorded and stored for reference by council personnel contemplating an upgrade for rating purposes.

The inspectors would be equipped with digital cameras, making it easy to provide helpful pictorial evidence of features which would increase the value of the property. They could demand entry to any room in the property, including bedrooms and bathrooms. Value-significant features could include a particularly nice view or any other amenity which might enhance one's lifestyle.

It has been reported that a government computer (another one!) is being set up at vast expense to store all the information so it can be accessed on an immediate basis. No doubt the claim that the information will be utilised to value properties for the imposition of estate duty is just a vile rumour!

It seems that, in pursuance of this scheme, officials have travelled abroad, even as far as Disneyworld, to learn how other jurisdictions have perfected this spying technique, in which aerial photography plays a significant part.

So, if you ever took comfort in the thought that you were master in your own house and that your private life was your own, think again. Big Brother may well be waiting to monitor your life in a way which your forebears would have found unbelievable – and insupportable.

IT'S A WISE CHILD…

'…that knows its own father', used to be the saying, but DNA has changed all that. In law, it is the natural father of a child who is liable to provide for it financially. At one time, a man who had treated a child who was not his as a member of his family would have been liable to pay maintenance for that child to his ex-wife after a divorce, but this no longer applies.

DNA test results are now said to be 99.9 per cent accurate, so a positive result will be relied upon as proof of paternity by the Child Support Agency and by family courts.

A non-resident parent can dispute paternity, but will be required to produce DNA evidence in support of his case. No-one can be compelled to submit, kicking and screaming, to DNA testing, but a potential father's refusal to co-operate can be taken as indicative of his belief that he is, in fact, the father.

Statistically, several thousand non-resident parents are men who are identical twins. A DNA test cannot normally differentiate between identical twins. The Child Support Agency has reported several cases annually where the men tested have a twin, and are denying paternity. These cases are referred to the court for a declaration of parentage, with a request that the other twin be made a party to the proceedings. DNA profiling would then be carried out on both men. Where either twin, or both, refuse to co-operate and provide evidence and information, it will be left to the court to decide paternity on the balance of probabilities.

Children born as the result of artificial insemination by donor are an exception to the rule that the father must maintain his child financially. Until recently donors were protected by anonymity. However, experience showed that the anonymous nature of the process could lead to problems, both practical and emotional, for the child so conceived.

From a practical viewpoint, children conceived by artificial insemination would have remained in ignorance of the genetic or medical history of their fathers, which, on occasions, could lead to avoidable medical risks. Perhaps, even more importantly, we all share an instinctive desire to know the details of our own family history. When the identity of one parent is cloaked behind an impenetrable curtain of anonymity, the child could suffer from genuine and damaging feelings of lack of self-worth. One young woman in this situation graphically described herself as 'a product, rather than a person'.

As a result, donors are no longer able to remain anonymous, so their children will now be able to obtain information about their paternity. Predictably, this change in the law has already led to a decrease in the numbers of men willing to participate in artificial insemination.

It's not only mothers who seek declarations of paternity. Former government minister David Blunkett famously and successfully established that he was the father of a disputed child. It has been estimated that as many as 25 per cent of children may not be the children of men who suppose themselves to be their fathers, so it can truly be said that 'it's a wise father…'

COMMON LAW MARRIAGE

The first thing you need to know about common law marriage is that there's no such thing. Never has been. And yet the myth persists. Surely, the argument goes, if a man and woman have lived together for a certain number of years, exactly as if they had been a married couple, they eventually get the same rights as married couples? The hard truth – particularly for women – is that they don't.

It doesn't matter how long they have lived together or if their friends and acquaintances – even their children – have always believed them to be married. If they don't have a marriage certificate, they are not entitled to the same treatment by the law if they separate.

The government has been tinkering with the idea that non-married cohabiting couples should have some rights analogous to those who are married. Gays and lesbians have now been given similar legal rights if they register their civil partnerships. This means that they are in a better situation than a man and woman living as husband and wife.

Many people say, 'What difference can a piece of paper make? We don't need it. We're in love and we'll be staying together without going to church, chapel, synagogue or register office…'

Cold statistics do nothing to validate this approach. The average non-married heterosexual relationship now lasts about two years. Even the average marriage only lasts ten. But when a marriage breaks down the courts have the power to make orders for spousal maintenance, if appropriate, for division of any capital and for the disposal of any property. Even pensions – and they can be the most valuable asset in the family – can be divided at the end of a marriage.

Among the problems the legislators will have to tease out, when it comes to giving non-married heterosexual couples the kind of rights which married couples have, is the definition quandary. How long would they have to have lived together? Would it be a shorter period if they had children? Until they find the answers to some of these questions, a change in the law which gives the same rights to couples who merely cohabit is unlikely.

What is glaringly obvious in these days of belief in equality of the sexes is that – as seems to happen with regrettable frequency – it's the women who most often get the rough end of the deal. The man will probably be the superior earner, with the superior pension provision.

If they have children, the woman will probably be the one who has sacrificed her career opportunities to bring them up. Had they been married, the court could take all these matters into account in determining what would be a fair division of their assets. Unmarried, she can forget it.

So, if you're a woman thinking about moving in with your partner without 'the benefit of clergy', as they used to say, do think hard about insisting on a legal agreement defining what your rights will be in the event of separation. It's unromantic certainly, but it's a wise form of insurance.

I CAN USE REASONABLE FORCE AGAINST CRIMINALS

Certainly, you can legally use reasonable force to protect yourself or your property if you are under threat of crime. The law is quite clear about that. Anyone can use reasonable force to protect him- or herself or others, or to carry out a citizen's arrest, or to prevent a crime. The snag lies in that word 'reasonable'. One person's idea of what is reasonable force can be, in the opinion of another, an excessive reaction to the provocation offered by the criminal.

Tony Martin thought that he was using reasonable force when two burglars attempted to steal antiques from his isolated Norfolk property. He used a shotgun. The unfortunate result was that one burglar was killed and the other was wounded in the leg. Many people were astounded when Tony Martin was charged with murder and convicted. On appeal, this was reduced to manslaughter, but he spent several years in prison. The wounded burglar was sentenced to imprisonment for 20 months, but issued a claim for £15,000 damages against Mr Martin, on the grounds that the wound had disabled him. There was every chance that he would have succeeded in this claim, had he not been photographed walking and cycling. Similar claims by other burglars have been successful.

So, when you are considering using reasonable force against someone who breaks into your property, it is best to bear the story of Tony Martin in mind. According to the Crown Prosecution Service, which has issued guidelines jointly with the Association of Chief Police Officers, 'wherever possible you should call the police'. Sound advice, no doubt, but a bit impractical when in the grip of the terror and urgency of a confrontational situation.

Reassuringly perhaps, the guidelines say that you are 'not expected to make fine judgments over the level of force you use in the heat of the moment'. If you 'honestly and instinctively believe' that what you are doing is necessary, that would be the strongest evidence that you acted lawfully and in self-defence. This is still the case if you use something to hand as a weapon. You don't even have to wait to be attacked. If you are in your own home and in fear for yourself or others, you can use defensive force.

This is all very well, as far as it goes. The real problem is that you will be reacting in a split-second situation. How are you expected to weigh up whether the force you use will be found to have been reasonable in future court proceedings which may be brought against you?

What it all seems to boil down to is that the definition of 'reasonable' depends on the individual circumstances of each case. Not much consolation, you may think, for Tony Martin and others who have found that the force they chose to use when under threat fell on the wrong side of that legal definition.

TWELVE GOOD MEN AND TRUE

If we're accused of a serious crime, we're all entitled to a trial by jury, are we not? Don't be too sure. Trial by jury, the bulwark of protection of the rights of the individual against the might of the state, has been a prized feature of our legal system since the barons took on the power of the monarchy and proclaimed the Magna Carta.

It was Shakespeare who coined the phrase '12 good men and true' to describe the panel of non-lawyers charged with the findings of fact in any criminal trial. The phrase '12 persons of different sexes' doesn't have quite the same ring to it, but juries have moved with the times and the emancipation of women has ensured that the jury box is no longer an exclusively male preserve.

The jury trial, together with other aspects of our common law, has been exported to a wide variety of court systems all over the world. You might have thought that it was something we could be proud of – an unassailable national treasure. This is not, however, the view of the government. A sustained attack on the jury system has been a feature of legislative proposals since the Labour party took office. So far, they have not been successful, but the arguments are insidious.

The attack, which is two-pronged, has been focused on complex fraud trials, which may take up months or, in some cases, years of court time. Few members of the general public can afford to sacrifice such prolonged periods, however public-spirited they may be. The second prong concerns the ability of jurors to

comprehend and follow the evidence offered in such marathon courtroom productions. No-one, apart from the members of individual juries themselves, knows what goes on in the jury room, since their deliberations should be conducted in total secrecy. But the argument propounded is that unqualified jurors can lose the plot and are consequently unwilling to convict.

It cannot be denied that in such cases these arguments must carry a good deal of weight. The unfortunate 12 who found themselves bogged down in one corruption trial for 21 months provide a terrifying example of what can happen. They would undoubtedly give wholehearted support to any move designed to avoid such an occurrence in the future.

But the concern is that abolition of juries for complex trials will be just the thin edge of the wedge. The government is keen to make inroads into the rights of the accused to opt for jury trial for all but the gravest crimes. Summary jurisdiction is cheaper; the reduction of cost is always a high priority.

The trouble is that, once such a right has been lost, it will be irrecoverable. So don't let's allow them to throw out the judicial baby with the bath water.

PRIVILEGE – WHAT PRIVILEGE?

When I consult a lawyer or my accountant what passes between us is totally confidential, right?

Wrong. Until comparatively recently, it was an established and cherished principle of law in this country that communications between a client and his or her solicitor, accountant or other professional adviser were 'privileged', which meant that the exchanges were entirely private. No professional could be required to disclose any information the client might have shared in the course of that relationship.

In many ways, it seemed to make a lot of sense, since people could be entirely frank about their finances, while seeking and receiving appropriate advice. Almost invariably, that advice would have been strongly in favour of the client making a voluntary disclosure of any irregularity, in his or her own interests (to the Inland Revenue, for example). But the details of any confidence of that nature were confined to the two parties involved. That was until 2002, when the Proceeds of Crime Act came into being, closely followed by the Money Laundering Regulations of 2003.

Considering the huge impact which these measures have had on the way in which professionals are now obliged to approach their clients, it seems astonishing that more fuss was not made about their provisions when the Act was going through Parliament. What they mean, in short, is any professional who becomes aware, in the course of dealing with a client, that the client is misleading or attempting to mislead the Inland Revenue is under a legal obligation to blow the whistle on him or her to the authorities.

Failure to do so leaves the professionals open to criminal charges and conviction, which doesn't exactly help them with regulatory bodies like the Law Society, and in all probability must amount to the end of their professional careers. Some found to be in breach of the legislation have already been sentenced to terms of imprisonment.

Most people are unaware that money laundering offences apply to all citizens. If you know or suspect that someone has acquired, retained, used or controlled criminal property by or on behalf of someone else, and you don't report it, you will be guilty of a criminal offence yourself. This is why banks have become so jittery about any unusual payments into your account, and will demand to know exactly where they came from.

You must have noticed the irritating insistence that you have to produce everything from your passport to two recent utility accounts and a bank statement addressed to you if you want to do anything from purchasing a property to getting hold of a senior citizen's bus pass. You can put all that down to the money laundering regulations.

Like it or not, we have to live with the new rules. Probably the only privileged conversations nowadays take place in confessionals and who knows for how long they will be allowed to remain confidential?

I CAN'T BE TRIED TWICE FOR THE SAME OFFENCE

For centuries the 'double jeopardy' rule wouldn't let anyone be prosecuted twice in the criminal courts for the same offence. The ancient defences which could be put up, on any occasion when there might be an attempt to do so, were known as 'autrefois convict' and 'autrefois acquit' – derived from the Norman French in use from the time when William the Conqueror ruled England.

'Jeopardy' means a real risk, in this case the danger of the punishment which might follow conviction. The rule was seen as an appropriate safeguard against putting someone through the trial process a second time, when he or she had already been acquitted – or indeed convicted – of the specific crime alleged.

But, as with so many long-cherished traditions, all that has changed. In 2003, the Criminal Justice Act provided that, in a case where there is 'compelling new evidence', the matter can be revived and the accused subjected to a retrial. No doubt the advances in DNA identification techniques have been a factor in the decision to turn the old rule on its head. The same Act empowered the Court of Appeal to set aside an acquittal in circumstances where new and compelling evidence had been obtained.

What the consequences of these fresh statutory powers will be is largely unknown, but one potential problem is pretty obvious. If a jury in the second trial is to be told that learned appeal judges took the view that the new evidence was so compelling that the defendant's

That parking case of yours dismissed in 1963 – we've got new evidence.

previous acquittal in a jury trial should be overturned, is it likely that the jurors will hesitate to differ from such an august opinion? In this case, there would surely be a real danger of the second jury giving a 'rubber stamp' verdict. The idea that the jury might be kept in the dark about the fact that there has been a previous trial is also fraught with difficulty.

It seems obvious that these new measures are unlikely to be invoked for petty crime. The expense and waste of court time would be likely to inhibit prosecutors from pursuing such applications. It looks highly probable that second trials will be confined to serious matters – murder and rape, for example. These cases tend to be widely reported, particularly when there is an acquittal. Presented with a history that triggers recollection of a media story, some jurors could no doubt put two and two together.

You can understand the argument that the perpetrators of serious crime shouldn't be allowed to get away with it, just because evidence which may have convicted them was not available at a previous trial where they had been acquitted. But if the jury in a second trial knows the whole story, will the accused get a fair hearing or will the case be unjustly weighted against him or her?

WE'RE JOINT OWNERS, SO WE EACH OWN HALF

You and your spouse, or live-in partner, own your home in your joint names, so each of you owns one half of its value. Actually, you might or you might not. It all depends on which kind of ownership you have.

Incredibly, there are two kinds, both described as 'joint ownership' but, in law, meaning completely different things. To create even more confusion, the different types are described as 'tenancies', although they are not rented. Just don't bother your head with that – it's going to take all of your concentration to learn the difference between the two.

In a joint tenancy, the owners do not have specified shares in the property. If one of two partners dies, the other becomes the outright owner. Because the shares are not defined, the person who inherits the estate of the one who dies will not inherit any part of the value of the property; that partner's share has gone to the other joint owner.

However, in a tenancy in common, each owns a share of the property. The shares are decided by the owners, either at the time of the purchase, when they can be registered, or by subsequent agreement. Failing agreement, a court would take contributions by each to the value of the property as a guide.

One of the crucial differences between a joint tenancy and a tenancy in common is that tenants in common each keep whatever his or her share may be. If one dies, the share will be a part of that person's estate.

Confusing? It gets worse.

If you are married to each other, or have registered your gay relationship, and you divorce (or seek a dissolution), the court has the power to override whatever your interests in the property may be and to make any order about the property that it considers fair in all the circumstances of the case. So your share could be transferred to your wife, husband or gay partner, whatever the former legal position might be.

If you are in a live-in relationship and you separate, the court does not have similar powers to deal with property. In the absence of any evidence of an agreement about shares, it will determine your interest on the basis of financial or other substantial contributions, such as work on structural alterations.

Complex, eh? But cheer up, you really only need to take away one thought at the end of all this. Whatever type of joint ownership you have, it's essential to clarify what your shares in it should be. It would probably be worth talking to a lawyer about having a legally binding agreement drawn up, to avoid a lot of subsequent heartache.

I WROTE THE BOOK SO
I GET THE ROYALTIES

It will come as no surprise to any author to read that this is not quite so simple. If, for example, you are the author of a self-help book, you will probably wander into your local public library on a fairly regular basis, just to check whether your book is on the shelves or not. The last time I checked, they had 13 copies of my self-help book listed on the library computer.

Good news, you might think. You couldn't be more wrong. The book was obviously popular, but people were not buying it. Either they were going to the library and taking a copy out in order to photocopy at home the bits that interested them, or they were using the photocopier in the library.

And that's legally permissible, as long as only one copy is taken for research or for private use. If you have had the foresight to register your book with the Public Lending Right organisation, however, you will get the princely sum of 5.57 pence every time the book is taken out. You get nothing if it's copied in the library.

Copyright law is supposed to help authors, songwriters, composers and others who produce creatively to protect their interest. But there are so many loopholes in the protection net that creative people could be forgiven for being slightly cynical about the whole system.

Giving members of the public the right to copy parts of your book does seem a touch unfair. Even more unfair

is the time limit on the protection of your ownership of your work. For literary, dramatic, musical or artistic works, you have 70 years from the end of the year of your death. Why should your heirs only enjoy them for a limited time? If an author happens to die young, the period during which copyright lasts will be even more curtailed. Where's the justice in that?

If you think that authors are hard done by, just spare a thought for singers and musicians who record popular music. Their protection lasts for only 50 years from the end of the year in which the work was recorded. You might not feel particularly sorry for someone like Paul McCartney or Cliff Richard, whose success has netted them millions and who continue to earn through writing and/or performance. But what about the aging performers who have enjoyed only fleeting success in their teens, perhaps having recorded one solitary hit which reached the charts and is still being played regularly? When they are in their sixties and at their most financially vulnerable, any income from those performances will dry up.

Why should ownership be limited at all? If you are a sculptor or an artist, no-one is going to claim that, after an arbitrary period, your heirs should be deprived of the right to own a statue or painting.

At the very least, why not make it 100 years?

MARRIAGE ISN'T A MEAL TICKET FOR LIFE

That certainly summed up the attitude of the courts over many years when they considered what should be the appropriate financial provision for wives after divorce. But in May 2006, the law lords comprehensively ditched the watchword, when they ordered a wealthy man to make annual maintenance payments of £250,000 to his ex-wife, to continue 'for as long as she needed them', unless circumstances changed to the point where the husband would be entitled to apply for a variation.

This case, together with a concurrent House of Lords decision that another wealthy husband must provide a lump sum of £5 million to his wife of less than three years, has sent a chill through the ranks of high earners. Already some solicitors are advising such clients to think again rather than rushing into matrimony.

Some high-flying lawyers are advocating prenuptial contracts, which are very popular with the wealthy in the United States, where they are legally binding. But our family courts have jealously guarded their right to examine the financial situation at the time of breakdown, taking all the circumstances into account, in order to reach a fair allocation of the matrimonial assets.

In England and Wales, a prenuptial contract will be given the weight which the court considers appropriate. If the parties were not separately legally advised, it may count for very little. Even when separate lawyers have been instructed to draw it up, its weight with the court will diminish according to the length of time which has elapsed since the date when it was signed.

For many people, the idea of making provision for divorce before the marriage ceremony takes place could seem a bit off-putting. In a letter to *The Times*, one clergyman declared that he would not perform a marriage if he knew of the existence of a prenuptial contract.

In some ways, you can see his point. Couples entering the married state generally do so in the hope and expectation that theirs will be a partnership for life. For one partner to attempt to limit any future financial liability should things not turn out as anticipated, is surely to put rather a damper on the romantic aspect of the marriage?

The barrister for the husband ordered to pay £5 million is reported to have made the rather unfortunate comment that it would have been cheaper for his client to have run his wife over in his car, causing serious injuries, financial compensation for which would have amounted to less than the sum awarded. This suggests to me the possibility that counsel may have been repeating an observation made by his client – not always the wisest thing to do in the context of a bitter matrimonial dispute.

However, at least the courts are being even-handed. On the day following the judgment of the law lords, a husband succeeded in getting a substantial lump sum from his seriously rich ex-wife. So these decisions are not all doom and gloom for husbands.

WE WERE ROBBED!

Not if you were burgled, actually. Both are thoroughly unpleasant experiences, and many people tend to use the terms 'burglary' and 'robbery' as though they were interchangeable. Legally they are two separate and quite distinct offences, however. The crucial distinction lies in whether there has been an element of violence, or a threat of violence.

The burglar is guilty of the crime if he or she enters your property unlawfully, with the intention of stealing or committing some other offence. He or she has to be a trespasser, in other words, someone who comes into your home without invitation or permission.

In one curious case the entry was effected by a man wearing nothing but a pair of socks. Intent on raping the female occupant of an upstairs bedroom, he had climbed a ladder up to her windowsill. Events then took a rather surprising turn when she invited him to come in.

At his trial for burglary, it was not clear whether the invitee was poised on the sill outside the window or had already climbed on to the sill inside the room at the point when the invitation was given. If he had been outside, the invitation would have transformed his status as a trespasser into that of guest (or, at best, licensee), which meant that he could no longer be convicted of burglary. Law students have found this a fascinating topic for debate ever since: if any part of him had

actually been over the sill, he would have remained a burglar.

Another would-be burglar was in the process of gaining entry, having broken a shop window in order to do so. He became trapped by his neck and couldn't move for fear of injuring himself. His feet were on the ground outside the shop, and only his head and right arm were inside. He tried to argue in court that he hadn't really entered the property because he couldn't have stolen anything in his predicament. This ingenious argument was rejected and the court found him guilty of burglary, on the ground that part of him had certainly entered the shop and he was there intending to steal.

Robbery is an even nastier offence and is punishable with maximum severity. A robber steals from you and in order to steal, immediately or at the same time uses force or threatens you with force. Common examples today are muggings for mobile phones, carjacking and robbery from people using cash machines. Robbery is committed by a wide range of offenders, from sophisticated criminal gangs to playground bullies.

But the football fans who grumble so vociferously that they have been 'robbed' when a referee hands a player a red card or disallows a questionable goal have no legal basis for their complaints. They haven't even been burgled!

I WANT MY NAME CLEARED

If you are accused of something which you haven't done, it is a wholly natural reaction to want to prove your innocence. In criminal cases – unless you are unfortunate enough to be an alleged terrorist – it is still a cherished principle of our law that you are innocent until proved guilty. If you are not convicted of the crime with which you have been charged, you can leave the court without a stain on your character.

Unfortunately, things are not quite so simple in the civil courts. To begin with, the test in a civil case is set at a considerably lower level than that for a criminal trial. In a criminal trial the court has to be satisfied of the guilt of the defendant 'beyond reasonable doubt'. The test in civil cases is 'the balance of probabilities'.

To take a fairly common example of what can happen, in a dispute between separated parents, an allegation may be made by the mother of a young child that the father has been sexually abusing the child during periods of contact.

It is only in relatively recent times that it has been acknowledged that many children in our society suffer sexual abuse, and that the abuser is often a member of the child's own family. It is good that this, once unmentionable, fact of life can now come into the open. Every child deserves protection, particularly from such abuse – the psychological consequences of which can be horrific and lifelong.

There is considerable debate about whether the publication of details of cases has increased the incidence of child abuse, or whether it has always existed at its present level. The availability of child pornography, in particular on the internet, may have contributed to the problem. The answers to these questions are unknowable.

What is sadly true is that some mothers, locked in bitter dispute with their former partners, have resorted to making false allegations with the intention of ensuring that fathers no longer see their children. When these allegations were first being made, about 20 years ago, a whole phalanx of self-appointed 'experts' appeared in the family courts, invariably supporting the mother's accusations, bolstering her case with intrusive cross-questioning of the child, often recorded on video film.

Happily, family judges are more aware now that, where there is a history of maternal opposition to contact, allegations of this nature should be treated with a considerable degree of reserve.

But family lawyers are all too familiar with the distraught father who demands that his name should be 'cleared' by the court. Tragically, it can't really work like that. A civil case is not a trial of guilt or innocence. The balance of probabilities may convince the judge that there is no truth in the allegation, but he or she is not in a position to declare 'this man is innocent'. A decision that the child should continue to have unsupervised contact with the father will have to be enough.

HOW CROSS SHOULD EXAMINATION BE?

We're all familiar with the scene. The barrister, resplendent in wig and gown, subjects the shrinking witness to a fusillade of aggressive and hostile questions, allowing him or her no sufficient opportunity to consider a reply, mocking the replies which do come out, only desirous of calling attention to the forensic brilliance of his or her performance. We've seen it a thousand times – in films and on television – and very exciting viewing it makes too.

But real courts in England and Wales are not like this, or they shouldn't be, although American courts, and those of some other jurisdictions, seem to permit the sort of histrionics which would be frowned on by our judiciary.

Rather than the showy pyrotechnics of fiction, it's meticulous preparation of the case which is the secret of successful cross-examination. The skilful barrister will lead a witness gently along a well-mapped path, beginning with seemingly innocuous questions which are easy to answer and apparently conceal no danger. At the climax of this exercise the witness will be faced with the question to which all of his or her answers have been directed; if he or she has not been telling the truth, the witness will be trapped into having to make the last admission he or she would want to make.

But that can only be achieved if the witness is attempting to hide something or is trying to mislead the court. An honest witness cannot be shaken, however skilled the interrogator.

...the truth, the whole truth and nothing like what you see on American TV –

Shouting at a witness, bullying or attempting to browbeat is not, unfortunately, completely unknown even in our courts, but counsel behaving like this will usually be rebuked by the judge. In any event, such conduct will do little to help the case being put forward by the lawyer concerned. Juries in criminal trials are unimpressed if they believe that witnesses are being badly treated. Judges, whether they are hearing criminal or civil cases, are likely to be irritated by legal representatives whose behaviour oversteps the mark.

So, if you have to give evidence in a case, how should you prepare yourself? Going into the witness box promising to tell the truth and nothing but the truth, is a scary experience for anyone – and that includes lawyers, I can assure you. You will be a very cool customer if you don't immediately find yourself in a state of considerable apprehension.

Take a deep breath, listen carefully to what you are being asked, and reply as best and briefly as you can. Replies which don't directly address the question, or which go on for paragraphs, are liable to get a witness into trouble. Never try to be clever, and always be polite.

If you are telling the truth, it's most unlikely that this will not be clear to the court. An honest witness has nothing to fear from cross-examination. If you are not being honest, of course, giving evidence could be more tricky.

WHATEVER HAPPENED TO CHILD SUPPORT?

We all knew, didn't we, when the Child Support Agency (CSA) was set up in 1993 that it would ensure that non-resident parents – mostly fathers – would make financial contributions towards the support of their children? At least, that is what we were told.

Now you claim to have received no Child Support payments for how long?

Until then, maintenance payments for children had been fixed by experienced family judges, but it was considered by the Conservative government that this was not the ideal arrangement. Under the new dispensation, judges were rarely to come into the process; in their place the calculation of the appropriate sum was to be achieved by means of an algebraic formula, universally applied and from which there could be no deviation or appeal.

The problems soon manifested themselves. First, there were the mathematical calculations to be made – so complex that they bewildered many lawyers, let alone the unlucky parents who were the clients of the agency. Second, the formula was far too rigid – some fathers on low earnings couldn't afford to have contact with their children. Horrifyingly, there were suicides.

Then there was the ever-increasing backlog at the CSA. Countless numbers of mothers on low incomes saw little or no payments being made; at the same time their benefits were cut. A year after the CSA was set up it had fallen £112 million short of its £530 million collection target and it was taking on more staff.

Months later, an official report found it had made errors in 86 per cent of cases. When Labour came to power, CSA payments were to be simplified. A new £456 million computer system was installed. Unacceptable backlogs continued to mount. By April 2005, most CSA staff members were saying they wanted to leave, so unhappy were they with their training on the computer system. By November, Tony Blair was saying that the CSA was not properly suited to its task; it was spending £12 million annually chasing non-payments, but had only recovered £8 million.

The National Audit Office revealed that the Agency spent 70p to collect every £1. £3.5 billion remained uncollected since 1993. Reforms had cost £539 million but had made no improvements; in some instances matters had been made worse.

While these breathtaking sums were sliding into the black hole created by a combination of the agency's incredible inefficiency with the pathetic faith of ministers in setting up unimaginably wasteful computer programs, families were suffering. CSA telephone helplines remained unanswered. We'd reached the point where, clearly, something had to be done.

Now we have been told that the CSA is to be scrapped and replaced by a new and efficient system. Parents are to be asked to make their own agreements about financial contribution. Enforcement procedures are to be improved. The most deprived parents and children in our society could be forgiven for taking a sceptical view. Has nobody thought about bringing back the judges? They may not have been perfect, but at least things worked better when they were in charge.

FINDERS KEEPERS

Hunting for treasure is an extremely popular pastime, as a glance through the numbers of internet websites offering sales of metal detectors of every kind will confirm. But the maxim 'finders keepers' was never a true reflection of the legal position. Under old common law 'treasure trove' meant, for example, found objects made substantially of gold or silver which had been buried by someone who intended to recover them. The duty of the finder was to try to identify the original owner, or his or her heirs, so that the treasure could be returned. Even if the rightful owner couldn't be traced, the finder didn't automatically have the right to keep what had been found.

But common law tends to develop in a complex way. The increasing popularity of hunting for treasure necessitated a clarification of what should be the procedure, so the Treasure Act was passed in 1996 in an attempt to tidy things up, so far as England and Wales were concerned.

The statute defines 'treasure', but a non-lawyer could be forgiven for being left in some confusion. Basically, any object which contains at least ten per cent of gold or

silver and is at least 300 years old is treasure. Coins dating from over 300 years ago are treasure. Single coins will not normally be treasure, but a number of such coins deliberately hidden is known as a 'hoard' and will officially be treasure. Any object is treasure, whatever it is made of, if it is found in the same place as treasure. Human and animal remains, however, are not treasure, even if they are found with treasure.

If you fail to report a find that you believe or have reasonable grounds to believe is a treasure without a reasonable excuse, you may be imprisoned for three months or be fined up to £5,000, or both.

If you are in doubt, and you probably will be, you must report a find to the coroner, either within 14 days of finding it, or within 14 days after the day on which you realised that it might be treasure. You will then normally be asked to take your find to a local museum or archaeological body. If it turns out to be treasure, it may be purchased by a museum and you will get a price for it or it may be returned to you, if no museum wants it.

But your troubles may well not be over even then. If you found it on someone else's land, that person will have a claim too. If you were a trespasser, without permission to look for treasure, you could find yourself in a difficult position. If you did get permission, you and the landowner might come to an agreement about how the ultimate value of any find should be shared.

Finders keepers is consequently no longer true – if it ever was.

WE'VE GOT A MARRIAGE CERTIFICATE SO WE'RE MARRIED

You can't be too sure about that.

You plan your wedding, fix a date, choose caterers, decide where the reception is to be, buy the rings, argue over the guest list and how many bridesmaids you should have, shop for wedding gear and book your honeymoon. The original budget has to be stretched, and stretched again. The run-up to the big day always throws up unexpected snags, but somehow you survive every crisis; at last, the arrangements are in place and the appointed time has arrived.

Take a deep breath; nothing to worry about now. Family and friends foregather in festive attire. A few sentimental tears are shed, toasts are drunk, speeches are made, and the whole thing goes like a dream. You are married.

But look what happened in Essex. During a six-month period, between October 2004 and the end of March 2005, almost 200 couples plighted their troth at a register office in Hornchurch and were handed their marriage certificates. In April 2005, each of those couples received formal notice from the local council responsible for the venue, confessing that the council had forgotten to renew its licence for marriages during the period.

The oversight might well have gone unnoticed had it not been for a sharp-eyed cleaner at the register office. Moving a pot plant in the course of her duties, this observant woman spotted that the date on the council's licence had expired and duly reported her discovery to her employers.

There must have been some red faces on members of the council staff. The appalling result was that those couples were, in all probability, not legally married. It may sound amusing but it was anything but a joke for them. Lawyers warned that there could be serious consequences, with financial problems in areas such as inheritance tax, pensions, life insurance, joint mortgage arrangements, wills and birth certificates.

One couple attempted to marry, but the Registrar General, no less, intervened to warn that purporting to get married again would invalidate both ceremonies. Is it any surprise that they were bewildered and more than somewhat annoyed? No one knew of any precedent for the situation and the matter had to be referred to a High Court Judge.

He ruled that the couples were legally married because they believed that the venue was licensed. Some lawyers would question that decision. But it is unlikely to be appealed. Unless, of course, one or more of those couples would now prefer that their marriages had not taken place.

If there is a moral to this cautionary tale, it must be that, when planning your wedding, it may be a sensible precaution to request sight of the licence for the venue, just to check that it's in date.

Especially if you are hoping to get married in Essex!

I WANT MY DAY IN COURT

It is quite astonishing how many apparently sensible people insist upon instructing their lawyers that they 'want their day in court'. This will be in preference to discussing any negotiated settlement of their case. They will brush aside offers to settle as rubbish – the other side wouldn't be making proposals to settle if they had any confidence in their own case, would they?

Their certitude that their side of the argument is so manifestly correct and so compelling that no judge could possibly do anything other than to find in their favour is what drives them on. They visualise themselves at the end of the case, emerging from the court triumphant and completely vindicated, their opponents utterly vanquished and humiliated. They adamantly refuse to listen to any opinion or advice which does not precisely coincide with their conviction that there is no point of view other than their own. Attempts to reason with them are doomed to failure and pointing out the weaknesses in their case only inflames their determination to bulldoze their way through the doors of the court.

Some will go so far as to ignore a pre-trial indication by the judge, who may already be familiar with the

paperwork, that their case might be a matter which ought to be settled, perhaps through professional mediation. As mediation is above all a voluntary process, to which both sides must come willingly, legal advisers can do nothing to help clients with a stubborn cast of mind realise that the judge could be dropping a considerable hint that neither side is likely to get exactly what he or she wants if the matter is to be heard.

This attitude is particularly prevalent in the family jurisdiction. The breakdown of any once-loving relationship almost inevitably generates feelings of bitterness and a desire to get the better of the other party. A 'wronged' spouse is convinced that, once the court hears about the iniquities perpetrated by the other, the judgment will berate the culprit, who will be revealed in his or her true colours.

This view conveniently disregards the undoubted truth that the other spouse will be just as persuaded that right is entirely on his or her side. It also ignores the fact that bad behaviour by one or other side can only in the most exceptional cases be taken into account by a judge deciding a matrimonial case relating to children, property or finance.

Public funding – called Legal Aid in the past – is now only available to those litigants in the poorest of circumstances, which means that people who demand their day in court must have the funds to pay for it themselves. The costs of litigation are increasing all the time, so it will be an expensive exercise.

At the end of the day, the result will almost always be that neither side gets precisely what he or she was aiming for. Lawyers will be the only ones who are better off.

LAWYERS LOVE TO OBFUSCATE

There is a perception among the general public that lawyers deliberately use language incomprehensible to their clients in order to promote the mystery of their calling. In the past, this was undoubtedly true, especially when it came to their frequent use of Latin in court.

It was quite usual for Latin tags to be bandied about between the Bench and the Bar, with the hapless plaintiff or defendant left feeling a sense of total bewilderment. But good lawyers, even then, were not happy to see their clients sink under the weight of a language which most of them might not even have heard of.

Some decades ago a distinguished Irish advocate was representing a client from a deprived area in the country. At one point in the case, the judge hearing it intervened to remark, 'But surely, Mr So-and-So, your client is familiar with the maxim 'caveat emptor'?' The barrister bowed, 'Your Honour,' he replied, 'in the bogs of Arran, where my client comes from, they speak of little else.' Whether the judge resented the deserved rebuke which had been administered is not recorded.

Non nobis laude viburnum
Quidnunc per ipsum ubi infra
haec vires quodlibet mensae
Quandoquidem fortuna mihi tete
abstulit ipsum

Hic prandium...
...Heu miser
indigne frater
adempte mihi

The use of Latin in our courts is now actively discouraged. It is recognised that those who appear before judges have at least the right to be able to comprehend what is going on. If everything seems to be taking place at some point way over your head, you may think to yourself, 'Hang on. This is my case and I haven't the faintest idea what these people are talking about.' Or you might think to yourself in even stronger terms.

Even now, many words and phrases which commonly crop up in legal documents are those which you would never come across in the columns of the red-top newspapers. Hereinbefore, hereinafter, demesne, curtilage, restrictive covenant, easement, ancient lights, joint and several liability, stakeholder, inventory and schedule are just a few that come to mind. And you could come across every one of those and more in the pages of just one document!

It is now widely accepted that it is the duty of a competent lawyer to make sure that a full explanation in simple everyday language is given in respect of every unusual word, so that the client can clearly understand all the terms which may be involved in any transaction or matter in which the lawyer may have been asked to advise.

However, even those of us who are committed to making all the words as comprehensible as possible can still trip ourselves up. On one occasion when examining a witness, I referred to a reply she had given to a question from the opposing barrister. I began by saying, 'You told my learned friend…', only to be interrupted by a plaintive wail from the witness box, 'Sorry, I don't know who your friend is!'

Served me right for being pompous.

THE MAJESTY OF THE LAW

Rather an out-of-date concept this. The expression used to imply a certain respect for the judiciary, which certainly did exist in the past. Today, judges are wearily becoming accustomed to virulent and largely uninformed criticism, not only from the media, which might be anticipated, but in recent times even from government ministers. The convention that the lawmakers would refrain from sniping at those responsible for administering the law has disappeared. Judges, unable to make any reply, let alone defend themselves, are now fair game.

On the lighter side, the majesty of the law is supposed to be made manifest in the robes and wigs donned by everyone from the Lord Chancellor (now about to be extinct, of course) down to the humblest junior barrister.

For a practitioner, making sure you have a set of clean starched bands to wear in court is almost as important as remembering to bring your notebook or, nowadays, your laptop. As a callow pupil I was sent to sit behind the head of my Chambers in an important case. I arrived in plenty of time, fortunately, as it turned out. 'Your bands,' he mouthed disapprovingly. What could he mean? They looked perfectly OK to me. But no. A minor member of the Royal Family had died and special mourning bands, known as 'weepers', had to be worn. I sprinted to a legal outfitter in Chancery Lane, arriving back, breathless and slightly dishevelled, but correctly attired, as the court rose to greet the judge.

Few London sights are more impressive than the procession of judges into the Royal Courts of Justice in

They felt it was time to update their image for the annual procession.

the Strand, which heralds the opening of the new legal year each autumn. More amusing is to watch them arrive to disembark from ordinary private coaches at the procession's point of departure. They have been attending the annual Lord Chancellor's Breakfast (actually, more of a lunch) in Westminster – whatever will it be called when we have no Lord Chancellor?

However, since my discovery that, in the past, male High Court Judges and Queen's Counsel wore suspender belts to keep up their silk stockings, their dignity has been a little diminished for me. The invention of tights has at least dispensed with that uncomfortable necessity.

Some people consider that the panoply of robes should be abolished as anachronistic and that lawyers in court should dress like everyone else. Curiously enough, in the House of Lords, the highest court in the land, the law lords sit to hear arguments in ordinary lounge suits, although everyone else is conventionally wigged and robed. The informality of dress adopted by the members of that august tribunal does not in the least detract from their authority.

So maybe it's just sentimentality to take the view that getting rid of the robes and the wigs would mean the removal of one more valuable tradition, when we already seem to have lost so many. They do have one inestimable benefit though: no-one who has encountered you in court will recognise you outside in the street.

SNACKING AT THE WHEEL

We all know, don't we, that it's a criminal offence to use a hand-held mobile phone while you are driving? But how many of us are aware that eating and drinking while we're at the wheel can also lead to a criminal charge?

It's very tempting, especially on a long and monotonous motorway journey, to reach for an apple, a banana or a sweet in order to provide ourselves with a welcome and refreshing distraction, even to renew flagging energy levels. Similarly, if the day is unseasonably warm, you may be in the habit of keeping a bottle of water or a can of coke within easy reach so that you can take a swig whenever you become thirsty.

Many drivers take the view that keeping snacks and drinks within reach on a long journey is a sensible precaution. Some believe that you are improving your concentration by helping yourself to refreshments when your attention begins to flag. But you may perhaps recall the case of the unfortunate nursery nurse fined £60 for holding an apple in her hand while negotiating a bend on the road. In evidence, police produced a video, shot from one of their helicopters – a real-life example of Big Brother watching you. Putting fellow road users at greater risk was the lorry driver who, absorbed in consuming a packet of crisps, steered through a mini-roundabout using only his elbows on the wheel. He was fined £250.

Consuming food or drink while you are driving can result in your being prosecuted for driving without due care and attention or for failing to be in proper control of your vehicle. If you are involved in an accident while eating or drinking, you can be charged with careless or even dangerous driving.

Research carried out at Brunel University found that 25 per cent of drivers are still risking penalties by using a mobile. It seems that, in contrast, 75 per cent of us choose to eat or drink something. In one test 26 volunteers were asked to drive a Ford Mondeo simulator on an urban road, once without eating and once while eating from a bag of wrapped sweets or drinking bottled water. The drivers were slowing down while doing so, but when the simulator showed a pedestrian suddenly stepping into the road, a significant variation in the rapidity of the drivers' responses was noted, leading to the conclusion that eating and drinking had impaired their ability to react to other events.

It is true to say that there is not yet a specific offence of snacking at the wheel on the statute books, but it may only be a matter of time. Even so, it could be a sensible practice to pay heed to all those motorway injunctions not to drive when you are tired, and just take a break at the next service station in preference to unzipping a banana.

MY OFFER FOR THE HOUSE HAS BEEN ACCEPTED SO...

…I have the right to buy it. You might imagine so, if you had never heard of gazumping, which is an ugly word for an ugly practice, still permissible in England and Wales.

What happens is that someone makes a better offer for the property you have chosen. The seller, despite having agreed to take your offer, then passes you by and goes for the higher figure. To your horror, you find that the increased offer has been made through the very estate agent who negotiated your purchase. This may not be quite the sharp practice it seems, because estate agents are legally bound to inform vendors of any offers that have made – and, of course, the higher the price paid the more the agent's commission will be.

If you are gazumped, you will, in all probability, have more than your thoroughly understandable disappointment to contend with. You may have expended a considerable amount of money on a professional survey of your prospective purchase and/or on legal fees. There will be no reimbursement for these expenses. Moreover, you may have put your own home

on the market and agreed to a sale on the basis that you had found what you wanted.

The agreement to buy and sell does not become binding until contracts have been exchanged between the seller's solicitors and your own. The truly nightmare situation, which must be avoided at all costs, occurs when you have exchanged contracts with your purchaser and you yourself are gazumped because contracts have not been exchanged on your purchase.

You may have to move in with family or friends when your purchaser takes over on the agreed date. If you don't have anybody who can help you out who lives in a convenient location, you may have to rent a property or move into a hotel while you wait to find something else. In either event, you will probably have to meet the cost of storing your furniture until you find a new home.

In view of all this, it is not surprising that moving house ranks only below bereavement and divorce when it comes to life's most stressful experiences. If you know anyone who has been gazumped, watch for steam coming out of their ears when they tell you about it.

It is possible to take out insurance against it happening to you, and some solicitors are prepared to draw up a 'lock-in' agreement which could take the form of both yourself and the seller paying a deposit of a small percentage of the purchase price. Should either side change his or her mind or try to change the agreed price without good reason, his or her deposit would be forfeited.

There are indications that the government would like to make gazumping illegal, which would be a solution welcomed by many who have suffered from this infuriating practice.

THEY'RE OUR CHILDREN SO WE CAN TAKE THEM ON HOLIDAY

Not if it's during term time and you don't get permission from the head teacher, you can't. Many parents do not take this prohibition all that seriously, and it may be that many head teachers turn a blind eye when parents fail to get the holiday sanctioned.

Parents' reasons for booking holidays during school terms are not purely selfish. Air fares and package holiday prices rocket as soon as the holidays start, so vacations cost that much more. Also, parents who are in employment have to compete with other parents in their workplaces for holiday time, if everyone is to be limited to the same few weeks on the calendar.

But few parents are aware that, since the Education Act of 1996, it has actually been a criminal offence to ignore the requirement to check with your children's headmaster or headmistress before removing them from the classroom for anything other than genuine illness, complete with a medical certificate to prove it.

One mother of three girls was prosecuted for taking her children out of school for a week, a holiday which included their participation in the finals of a dance competition, in defiance of their primary school head's refusal to agree that she could do so. The following term she took the girls on another unauthorised holiday, which she had won in a competition. It was also claimed that the children's attendance had been generally poor; absences had been attributable to medical problems, the mother's car breaking down or traffic jams which had made them late for the school register. However, the evidence was that all three girls had been assessed as above average in their school work.

The mother was prosecuted in the Magistrates' Court. The magistrates came to the conclusion that she had not failed to ensure that her daughters attended regularly. They commented that the mother should have exercised greater care in relation to holidays, but concluded that, on the whole, the absences had been justified.

Some of us might think that the magistrates exhibited a good deal of common sense, but that was not the view of the education authority, which appealed to the High Court. A High Court Judge and a Lord of Appeal decided that the magistrates had 'misdirected themselves' on the law. They only had to decide on an issue of strict liability – whether the children had failed to attend school regularly. They had not applied the correct statutory test. They were not entitled to decide whether the absences had been justified.

The case was sent back to the magistrates, with a direction that the mother should be found guilty. Because of the length of time which had elapsed since her crime had been committed, the appeal judges indicated that she should be given an absolute discharge, so she wasn't fined or put in prison. But she still has a criminal record.

Is it just me, or is that a bit draconian?

∾ MISCONCEPTION # THIRTY SIX ∾

WE'LL ALL HAVE IDENTITY CARDS SOON

Won't we? The Passport Office has already been renamed the Identity and Passport Service and has been equipped with one of those incredibly expensive computer systems so beloved of the government. In 1999, when the new requirements came in that babies and children should have their own separate passports, the extra work combined with computer problems resulted in a backlog of 565,000 applications. People desperate to get away formed long queues and 1,200 umbrellas were purchased for those unlucky enough to have their misery increased by having to stand in the rain.

In 2006 the new computer system was introduced, only to break down a matter of 20 days into its use, leaving a further 5,000 people stranded. Prime Minister Tony Blair, undaunted, reaffirmed that identity cards are 'a major, major issue' for the government. But other experts are not convinced that they should be.

The Commons Science and Technology Committee was concerned about confusion over what the scheme would entail, stating that it was crucial to increase 'clarity and transparency'. MPs were also sceptical about the official estimated annual running costs of £584 million, particularly in view of research at the London School of Economics, which estimates that implementation and running costs would total £10.6 billion to £19.2 billion over the first ten years. To add to the woes of the government, the Information Commissioner upheld two complaints that information about independent analysis of the progress of the ID project was unfairly shrouded in secrecy.

The Office of Government Commerce (OGC) is entrusted with carrying out regular reviews on all such high-risk IT enterprises set up by government. But the OGC is refusing to publish details of its findings.

Originally, we had been assured that identity cards would have been issued in respect of every citizen by 2008. Every card would have a biometric chip which would entail every adult having to provide fingerprints and submit to iris scans on their eyes. It seems increasingly unlikely that this target can be achieved. Tendering for contracts for this programme, which will run into multimillions, has been postponed.

It is now believed that the requirements may be dramatically simplified: possibly you will only have to provide prints of two fingers plus a digital photograph.

Considerable concern has been expressed about just what other information might be available to the government on that microchip, so this simplified card will be welcomed.

It is said that ID cards will help in the war against terror, but this argument has failed to convince many. Most of us already have forms of identification – our passports and driving licences both contain photographs. British potential terrorists will be able to apply for ID cards just like the rest of us. Is it really worth spending £19.2 billion on plastic ID in preference to more on education and the health service?

RAPE VICTIMS HAVE USUALLY ASKED FOR IT

Tragically, this seems to be a thoroughly entrenched view among the general public. Until recently it was a view reflected in the treatment of victims by the police. The fear of being treated with scepticism by officers deterred many victims from going to a police station.

It is to the credit of the police that victims are now generally shown gentleness and sympathy. In many stations specialist officers conduct their interviews in separately planned environments designed to provide a reassuring ambience. A booklet, which answers many of a victim's questions in clear language, has been issued by Sapphire – the organisation set up to improve the approach of individual officers to the problem. The anonymity of victims is now protected.

But the rape victim must endure a second ordeal, should the matter have to go to court. In the past, defence counsel was permitted to cross-examine the witness about her previous sexual history, but this is no longer the case. Yet the thought of having to re-live what has happened in the public arena of a criminal court is frequently one which puts victims in a state of terror.

When the matter does go to court conviction rates are not high. In particular, juries tend to be suspicious of 'date rape' allegations, where the accused is known to the victim who may have had consensual sexual relations with him in the past. They will also put into the balance any delay in reporting the crime.

The way the victim dresses or behaves can often affect the weight that the jury gives to the evidence. Girls who wear short skirts or revealing clothing are considered to have been 'asking for it'. If the victim has been drinking, there is even less chance of persuading a jury that a crime has really been committed. But women (and men) should be free to dress as they please, and to consume alcohol if they wish to do so, without thereby making themselves fair game to a violent criminal.

If a victim is in a drunken state, does it mean that consent can be assumed by an assailant? The complex question of 'legal capacity' to consent then has to be put before the jury. Definitions like this are difficult for lawyers and judges, let alone the man in the street.

The government issued a discussion paper on obtaining more convictions for rape. A possibility suggested was that expert psychological evidence might be called in cases where the victim had delayed reporting, since delay is explicable from a psychological viewpoint. But would that make much difference to the conviction rate?

As a result of the improvements, more rapes are now being reported; convictions, however, have not increased. It is the attitude of the men and women who make up the juries which needs to be changed if justice is to be done.

INHERITANCE TAX IS FOR THE WEALTHY

That was the idea once. The imposition of tax on seriously rich families seemed a good plan – it would cut them down to size thereby reducing their power and influence; at the same time it would increase revenue. As it turns out, these primary objectives have not been achieved. Wealthy people, with the expert help of tax lawyers and financial advisers, have been able to find ingenious ways around the problem of leaving too much money when they die. Their descendants have been able to hang on to the riches of their forebears.

At the same time a situation has been allowed to develop where inheritance tax is now hitting families of very modest means. At present, if you die leaving assets over a certain figure (currently £285,000), tax will have to be paid at the rate of 40 per cent on any sum in excess of this figure. The rise in house prices has meant that this tax now affects more people. The value of the average home today is £200,000 and an ever-increasing number of estates exceed the figure at which the tax comes into operation. Since the Labour government came into power in 1997, the revenue collected in inheritance tax has doubled, together with the number of estates on which it became due – 18,000 in 1997, 37,000 in 2005.

The government takes the view that people should not benefit from the 'windfall' of increased house prices. But the people who have purchased their own homes have done so with their own earnings, on which they have already paid tax. Inheritance tax has rightly been described as 'a tax on death'.

A large proportion of those whose estates will attract the tax are quite unaware of what the impact will be and would not even imagine that they might need the advice of tax experts on how they can avoid some or all of its impact. In any case, you need to be seriously rich to take advantage of these dodges.

One way to minimise the tax is to make cash gifts to children and grandchildren during your lifetime. These will not be included in your estate so long as you survive for seven years after the gift is made. But the new victims of inheritance tax have no liquid assets.

It is often only after death, when family members are left trying to cope with the aftermath, that they realise that they may have to sell the home in order to meet the demands of the revenue. A daughter, for example, who has cared for an aging mother in her parent's home, could, on the parent's death, be faced with raising a sum only achievable if she sells the property.

Inheritance tax is a form of stealth tax – a growing threat to ordinary citizens who have worked hard and paid their taxes all their lives, and have consequently been able to acquire their own homes. If the tax is not to be abolished altogether, there is a strong case for raising the threshold figure to the point where ordinary men and women will not be hammered.

HUMAN RIGHTS
ARE FOR EVERYONE

In our society we have long been justly proud of the fact that everyone has the same rights of citizenship. Other countries may have needed their Bills of Rights or their written constitutions, but from the time of the Magna Carta our unwritten constitution had provided protection for every citizen, without the necessity of setting it all out on paper.

However, we now have the Human Rights Act, which defines the various categories of right which each of us has in documentary form, set out in wordy and sometimes impenetrable paragraphs. But are we better off? Many people think not; even the government has come up against the provisions of its own legislation in the courts, much to the discomfort of ministers.

Three of our Home Secretaries, Blunkett, Clarke and Reid, with the support of the Prime Minister, have complained vociferously about judges who have been guilty of no greater fault than administering the law as it is. The Prime Minister went so far as to allege that the statute had empowered the judges to overturn an Act of

Parliament, apparently forgetting that his government had been responsible for enacting the provisions he now finds so unacceptable. Judges, of course, have to remain silent in the face of such public criticism.

In the light of all this, it is good news that the review of the UK Act and the European Convention on Human Rights by the Chancellor concluded that the law needed no amendment. However, to our shame, there is an increasing climate of opinion among members of the government and in the media which favours the notion that some of us are not really entitled to have our human rights respected. Convicted criminals serving terms of imprisonment, paedophiles and suspected terrorists are examples of those considered too beyond the civilised pale to be any longer regarded as human, so that they can be stripped of their legal rights with impunity.

To point out that this view represents the first step down a very slippery slope indeed will not find much favour with its supporters. Politicians and the red-top media were pressuring Lord Falconer to propose that the Human Rights Act be amended, even that we should remove ourselves from the ambit of the European Convention. To his eternal credit, Lord Falconer resisted the pressure and pointed out that amendment or repeal would make little or no difference to the decisions made in our national courts.

Let us hope that our judges will continue to defend the rights of even the most underprivileged and despised in our society, as has been their honourable tradition. Otherwise, who knows what inroads into rights which we ourselves take for granted might be made in the future?

FAMILY COURTS ARE SECRETIVE – AND THEY FAVOUR WOMEN

Militant organisations like Fathers4Justice have persisted in their campaigns against family judges to the point where many people believe that family courts are secretive, unaccountable tribunals, where judges invariably make their decisions in favour of wives and mothers. This could not be further from the truth.

Family judges have to operate in one of the most difficult and delicate areas of the law. Family disputes are not suitable for the court environment. They should be resolved by reasonable discussion between the parties, assisted, if necessary, by qualified professional mediators. Unfortunately, there are protagonists in the family courts who refuse to negotiate about their differences, or to consider mediation. There has to be some means of resolving these arguments. Family judges are landed with the job.

These judges make their decisions in accordance with the strict injunction that, in any case where children are concerned, it is the welfare of the children which must be paramount over all other considerations. When they observe this principle, it will usually be the mother who will get residence of the children, not because there is any prejudice against fathers, but simply because of the circumstances of the case.

Mothers are usually the main carers of children, particularly when the children are young. Fathers usually have jobs which make it impractical for them to have children living with them. Where financial resources are too limited to provide each parent with a home, the family home often goes to the mother, simply because she will be living there with the children. The father's interest in it may be delayed until the children have ceased full-time education, or his superior pension rights may be left untouched in recompense for his loss.

Having considered the interests of the children, the court will do its best to resolve issues in relation to property and finance in as fair a way as possible.

When there are disputes about the amount of contact a non-resident parent should have with his or her children, again it is the interests of the children that will be given prominence. Courts are anxious to ensure that children spend as much time with both parents as possible; if a parent is debarred from contact with a child, it will invariably be because there is some risk to the child in permitting contact.

The fact that family cases are not open to the public is a concern for the judiciary, as much as for disgruntled fathers. The reason for the confidentiality is to protect the privacy of the parties and, above all, of their children. The government is currently considering proposals for opening the doors of family courts to the public, while at the same time preserving the anonymity of those involved. Family judges would welcome this – it would inevitably make for a better understanding of their difficult role.

HEALTH AND SAFETY LAW PROTECTS US

The idea behind health and safety regulations was a good one, but exaggerated fears of breaching them have made us terrified of our own shadows. When schools are too nervous to take pupils on outings, when hospital wards ban flowers and parish picnics are cancelled on health and safety grounds, you begin to wonder where it will all end. Even the Health and Safety Commission (HSC) has become concerned about the timidity engendered as a result of its admonitions. We have reached the point where looking over our shoulders all the time is actually beginning to put us in danger of wrapping ourselves and our children in metaphorical cotton wool, to the extent that we have forgotten how to enjoy ourselves.

The Chair of the HSC has pointed out that some health and safety stories were 'actually myths'. The trouble is that it is difficult to distinguish the myths from reality. But it is undoubtedly true that people occasionally invoke health and safety law to justify unpopular decisions. An example of the hidden agenda in these situations is that it is cheaper to close a council playground with swings and climbing frames than to maintain it to a decent standard so that the facilities are in good repair.

Some schools are so wary of being taken to court by overprotective parents that games like conkers are banned, and the natural exuberance of children is too severely restricted. Children today are not as self-confident and independent as those of previous generations. To see primary school children walking unaccompanied to and from school is a rarity nowadays;

their parents at the same age were probably making the journey independently on foot as soon as they could be trusted to cross a road.

It is sad to see school playgrounds surrounded by impenetrable fencing, as so many are today. One can understand that there is a fear of unsuitable intruders gaining entry, but some of the precautions taken leave the premises looking more like prison camps than educational establishments.

Planned New Year's Eve celebrations in London have been cancelled in the name of health and safety, army bagpipers have been ordered to wear earplugs to stop them going deaf and Torbay council attached warning notices to the town's traditional palm trees explaining that the 'very sharp leaves…could cause injury to eyes or faces, if inappropriately placed'.

Apprehension about possible risks can be taken too far and it is welcome news that even those organisations responsible for ensuring health and safety are beginning to recognise this. One official said, 'I'm sick and tired of hearing that health and safety is stopping people doing worthwhile and enjoyable things. If you are using health and safety to stop everyday activities, get a life and let others get on with theirs.'

Sounds like common sense, doesn't it?

LEADING QUESTIONS

There is a lot of misunderstanding about leading questions. A politician being aggressively interviewed on the *Today* programme will sometimes accuse the interviewer of asking a leading question. People equate 'leading' with 'intrusive' or 'impertinent'.

In law, a leading question is none of these things. It is a question which a barrister puts to his or her witness and which suggests the answer to the witness. Counsel are not allowed to say to their own witnesses, for example, 'Isn't it right that you were at home on the night in question?' That would be leading the witness to an answer you wanted.

Conversely, if you are cross-examining, you can put the same question with perfect propriety because the person responding is not your witness but a witness for the other side.

Inexperienced barristers often fall into the trap of asking leading questions of their own witnesses and will very promptly be corrected by the judge. But lack of experience can leave you floundering. You ask the neutral question, 'Do you remember what happened on the night of February 2nd last year?' Your witness looks completely blank. All you can think of is to repeat the question, your eyes begging her to remember her statement. She doesn't.

This was the nightmare scenario for me on one of my first appearances in a divorce case in the High Court. The judge was a pleasant man but he had suffered a leg wound in World War II and couldn't sit comfortably, so had the rather disconcerting habit of prowling up and down in front of the Bench as the evidence was given. Observing the impasse between my client and myself and taking pity on me, he suddenly arrested his perambulations just below the witness in the box and pointed an accusing finger at her. 'You know what happened on the night of February 2nd last year,' he admonished her. 'Your counsel knows what happened. But the silly old judge doesn't know what happened.'

Miraculously, this intervention restored her memory and we were able to proceed.

In those days all divorce cases had to be heard in court. Undefended suits were heard at speed and were difficult to lose, since there was no-one on the other side.

But you had to prove that the respondent to the suit had been served with notice that the petition had been filed. A form, the acknowledgement of service, would be sent with the petition, which the respondent was required to sign and return. Counsel had to ask the petitioner to identify the respondent's signature.

One respondent had reacted by scrawling an extremely offensive word across the form, crumpling it up and throwing it in the rubbish bin, where his wife had found it. When the judge asked to see the acknowledgement I could only hand up the sorry result. 'I'm afraid it's unsigned,' I faltered.

The judge glanced at the obscenity and handed it to the usher. 'Never mind about that. Does the petitioner recognise the handwriting?' he enquired. Fortunately, she did.

CHILDREN SHOULD BE WARNED ABOUT STRANGERS

Every parent is conscious of the problem of child abuse in our society. In recent years paedophilia has become such a familiar concept that no-one could be unaware of its existence. Curiously, it is only over the last couple of decades that there has been so much discussion on the topic.

Some believe that it has always been as prevalent as it seems to be today. Others think that in the past it was so shameful that it was ignored, denied and kept hidden by society. Whatever the truth may be, there can be no modern parents who are not fearful that their child may become the victim of a paedophile. Many believe that the best way to protect their children is to warn them against having anything to do with strangers.

It is true, of course, that a stranger may approach your child hoping to get acquainted for some nefarious purpose; the approach may be made in a public place like a park or a cinema, very frequently it will be through the medium of an internet chat room. So it is certainly common sense to explain to your children that people they do not know should be treated with great reserve.

But parents should be aware of the dreadful truth that it's much more common for children to be abused by someone they know and trust – a family member or a family friend – than by a stranger.

So the sensible approach is to instruct your child from the youngest age about good touches and bad touches. If anyone at all touches certain parts of your child's body, your child should understand that a parent or teacher must be told.

It is eminently sensible to equip children with the ability to protect themselves in this way, but it has to be done without going over the top and scaring the child. Even adults can, on occasion, carry anxiety about abuse to unfortunate extremes.

We read about teachers who are afraid to comfort young pupils who have grazed their knees in the playground or are reluctant to put lotion on their foreheads to protect them from burning in the sun, fearful that these attentions may be misconstrued.

A child who runs to someone familiar expecting to be hugged will feel hurt and bewildered if the adult responds coldly, turning away from the enthusiastic approach.

However, it is understandable that adults have become conscious of the danger that ordinary gestures of affection are open to misinterpretation, particularly if the adult has a professional relationship with the child concerned.

We are in danger of quenching the natural spontaneity of children if they learn from such experiences that their affectionate overtures will be repulsed. But if we are bringing up a generation that has been taught to exercise a constant wariness of others, what will be the long-term effects on our children's ability to make relationships in the future?

I CAN CHOOSE MY HOSPITAL

Patient choice is the current watchword for our National Health Service. If you need hospital treatment, so it is said, all you have to do is to choose any hospital you like the sound of and a bed will be yours. Sound too good to be true? You may well be right.

In order to bring about this miracle of choice for everyone, the government has invested in yet another unimaginably expensive computer, not just any old computer either; this one is believed to be the largest civil computer project in the world.

It is intended to house the records of every NHS patient, and to be accessible to all general practitioners and hospitals. At its launch in 2002 it was estimated that it would cost £2 billion. This estimate has now risen to £15 billion and there seems little reason to imagine that it will not escalate further, as costs for these grandiose schemes so inevitably do. The widespread indebtedness affecting many NHS trusts is in no small measure attributable to the expense associated with their endeavours to implement the plan.

In December 2005 Oxford's Nuffield Hospital was reported to have run into 'major operational difficulties'

It's all part of patient empowerment. First you choose the hospital, then you choose the instruments –

when it began to set up the system. Patients who had been dropped from waiting lists or who were not being recalled to the hospital for treatment had apparently disappeared from the hospital's computer records.

Not terribly reassuring, that. The safety of a patient might easily be compromised in a situation where his or her medical history was inaccessible to doctors making decisions about how to treat him or her in an emergency.

The body set up to implement the system nationwide is called Connecting for Health. Unfortunately, the company appointed to provide software to this body has run into serious financial difficulties. It now seems highly unlikely that the government will meet its target date of 2008 for making all this fully operational.

Some of us, in any event, feel a certain amount of apprehension at the idea that we should be responsible for selecting the most appropriate hospital to treat any serious condition which might be visited upon us. What do we know of the relative merits or skills offered by the different options? Are we to rely purely on anecdotal evidence on how successfully – or otherwise – a particular surgical operation was performed, for example, on an uncle of a man we met in a pub? Or do we go for the hospital with the prettiest garden surrounding it, or the easiest one to reach by public transport?

Looked at in the cold light of day, none of these methods of hitting on the best hospital for my particular condition strikes me as being very reliable. Even if the government manages to get this mammoth system to work – and I wouldn't bet on it – I suspect that most patients will prefer to go for the old system, and fall back on leaving it to their general practitioner to make the choice.

∾ MISCONCEPTION # FORTY FIVE ∾

BIG BROTHER ISN'T WATCHING US

The nightmare scenario described in Orwell's *1984* predicted a time in the future when an all-powerful government would be able to spy on all its citizens, enabling it to control every aspect of their lives. Fiction, yes?

It couldn't happen here, could it? Just consider the creepy news that, totally without any warning or consultation, local authorities are putting concealed electronic bugs in our wheelie bins. This story broke when an indiscreet council official let it slip on a social occasion. Outraged ratepayers in his area discovered that the bugs had already been fitted under the lip of their bins, without any permission having been sought and in the absence of any publicity. It seems that half a million bins in the country have already been equipped with the bugs. It is anticipated that most local authorities will be installing the devices over the next couple of years.

Each bin will be given a number which will identify the household from which the rubbish comes. The gadgets transmit information about the contents of your bin to a central database which will hold records on the waste disposal habits of the residents at each address.

Officially, the bugs are being promoted on the basis that they will 'improve efficiency' and settle arguments between neighbours about wheelie bin ownership. But we can hardly be expected not to wonder about a wider agenda, particularly bearing in mind that the introduction of the project has been so cloaked in secrecy, with some councils debating the proposals in sessions closed to the public.

It is said that the bugs will be able to differentiate between waste which ought to be put out separately for recycling, and general waste. Waste can also be weighed as it is loaded on to the collection lorries. So it seems not unlikely that this information will be used to raise additional income for local authorities. Anyone who throws out too much rubbish, or recycles incorrectly, will be liable to a fine, an increase in rates or both.

There's no doubt that the Big Brother style of government is insidiously taking over our lives. We now have a legal responsibility to inform the Inland Revenue if we believe that someone we know is cheating on income tax returns.

People are being encouraged to snitch on their neighbours if they suspect that they are sneaking out at midnight to water their lawns. If you have a loyalty card at your supermarket, records are kept on your spending habits. The day may come when you could be penalised for buying foods loaded with excessive fat or sugar, or you could even risk a prison sentence for including cigarettes on your shopping list.

You think I'm exaggerating? Have a look under the lid of your wheelie bin.

ASBOs PROMOTE RESPECT IN SOCIETY

Anti-Social Behaviour Orders (ASBOs) are supposed to be the answer to many of the ills in our communities. The Respect agenda was intended to bring together central government, local agencies, local communities and, ultimately, every citizen, to work together to build a society in which we can respect one another.

It was anticipated that ASBOs imposed on persons guilty of anti-social behaviour would represent a vital contribution to this rather optimistic project. Disrespectful behaviour punishable by the administration of an ASBO would include throwing bricks through a neighbour's window, making offensive and threatening remarks, dumping litter and urinating in the street. You could no doubt add a few of your own particular gripes to the list.

We are all only too aware that our society is, in fact, characterised by a complete lack of respect, even for parents, teachers, senior citizens and people who suffer from a disability. As a rule, it is the younger generations who normally appear unaware of the very notion of respect for anyone, but mature and senior adults sometimes share their attitude, or are at least reluctant to interfere with objectionable behaviour for fear of being subjected to something even worse. It takes more courage than most of us possess, for example, to ask a youngster to remove his or her feet, usually clad in filthy mud-caked trainers, from the opposite seat on the train, or to remonstrate with a youth casually relieving himself on a suburban pavement.

The powers-that-be have correctly identified that the root cause of such behaviour arises in the home.

Parenting orders can be made in an attempt to instil some parental skills into the most disadvantaged family units. Parents can be made to take responsibility for the actions of children who are the subject of ASBOs. But when parents have to work anti-social hours in order to keep their families fed and clothed, is it fair to expect them to monitor a curfew which has been imposed on their children?

Statistics have been published for the numbers of ASBOs imposed, identifying the different areas of the country in which the orders have been made. Figures for the numbers of orders which have been breached have not been made available since 2003, however, when breaches were reported in 25 per cent of cases.

A surely unintended consequence of the imposition of the orders has been that in some areas, to have been subjected to an ASBO gives a young person considerable 'street cred' with contemporaries.

When the Respect Action Plan was launched it identified six strands to the plan: supporting families; a new approach to the most challenging families; improving behaviour and attendance in schools; activities for young children and young people; strengthening communities; effective enforcement and community justice.

Have you noticed much of that happening?

As the victim, I can expect justice

Not according to the Director of Public Prosecutions, you can't. In a speech delivered to lawyers and criminologists in March 2006, Ken Macdonald expressed grave reservations about the perception of victims and witnesses in criminal trials that more consideration was being given to the accused than to them.

This, he believes, has promoted the belief that justice is more concerned with the rights of criminals than with the law-abiding majority. The government is anxious to rebalance the system between law breakers and the law abiding.

Defence lawyers tend to cross-examine victims and other witnesses for the prosecution aggressively. Giving evidence in a criminal trial can often be experienced as an unpleasant ordeal by people who are themselves innocent of any crime. The British Crime Survey 2005–2006 found that 80 per cent of respondents thought that the system was fair to the accused, with only 36 per cent believing that it was fair to victims.

Some of the measures being considered to remedy the situation are to make violent criminals pay for medical treatment for their victims, making it easier for victims to sue for damages in the civil courts and curbing the discharge of defendants on technicalities. The automatic reduction of a sentence when a plea of guilty is offered may also be abolished.

It is hoped that 8,000 additional prison places will be available by 2012. In the meantime, overcrowding of existing establishments has resulted in sentencing guidelines indicating that shoplifters, even if they are repeating their offences, should not be sent to prison. Some prisoners are also expected to be given early release.

The Home Secretary wants recruits to the Parole Board to have had direct or indirect experience of the effects of crime, and victims may be given representation by an official from the Home Office when a prisoner convicted of a violent or sexual crime is being considered for parole. A pilot scheme at the Old Bailey and four Crown Courts permits victims to address the court about the effects of the crime, after the verdict but before the sentence is passed. The judge will not be influenced by this evidence, but it is difficult to believe that the practice will not lead to many appeals on the ground that he has taken it into account.

The proposals being made are untested, but could be given a cautious welcome. The trouble is that if you happen to live on a sink estate where you are subjected to vandalism and petty crime on a daily basis, you are not likely to be too reassured by the package.

Crime has been allowed to proliferate over the past decade. Many of us fear that the current concentration of policing on the terrorist threat can only mean that we will be increasingly at risk on the streets and in our homes as dangerous criminals go undetected.

MY PRENUPTIAL AGREEMENT GUARANTEES THAT I WON'T BE TAKEN TO THE CLEANERS

Unfortunately, not necessarily!

Prenuptial agreements, legal documents setting out what will be the division of the family assets should a marriage break down, are popular in the United States and some continental countries, where the terms remain binding and the courts are unable to interfere with what has been agreed.

Leaving aside the thought that to enter the state of matrimony with a canny eye on the exit may seem to some less than romantic, there's no doubt that wealthy brides and grooms who may be marrying beneath them financially are usually anxious to hang on to their riches should the relationship founder.

Requests for legally binding prenuptial agreements to be drawn up are consequently becoming more popular, and you will have no difficulty in finding a solicitor who will agree to draw one up for you.

The trouble is that our courts do not consider themselves bound by the terms of any such agreement. In hearing financial questions relating to divorce, a judge has the widest possible remit to look at all the circumstances of the case. He or she is, in fact, obliged by statute to take certain matters into account, such as the age and health of the spouses, the ability of each to earn a living and the standard of life enjoyed during the marriage. The needs,

obligations and responsibilities of each will also be considered before an adjudication is made.

If there is a prenuptial agreement in existence, this would clearly be one of the circumstances to which the judge would have to have regard. And if the marriage broke down within months of its celebration, there is no doubt that the terms of the agreement would be persuasive, because they would enshrine the beliefs of the parties as to what would be fair, agreed by them on a fairly recent date.

But as time passes, the prenuptial agreement is likely to be of less influence on the decision which is made. After a period of years, for example, changes will obviously have taken place in the circumstances of the couple. There may be children and the person who is to have them living with him or her will clearly have additional needs and responsibilities as a result. All sorts of other developments during the course of the marriage will also have an influence in the decision-making process.

So, if you are financially well off and take a pretty pessimistic view of whether your marriage will endure, you could certainly ask your intended to agree that a lawyer should be instructed to draw up a prenuptial agreement. What message that request may convey can only be imagined.

Just keep in mind that it's not the same as an insurance policy.

EASEMENTS MAKE PROPERTY OWNERSHIP EASIER

Easements sound gentle and emollient, as though they should make property owning easier, but this is usually pretty far from being the case. An easement is something which gives a property owner some right in relation to property owned by another person. You may care to know that, in legal terminology, the person with the benefit of the easement is called the 'dominant' owner and the person providing the easement is called the 'servient' owner. On the other hand, you probably couldn't care less.

So what are easements? They are too many and varied to enable the recitation of a comprehensive list. An example might be if you had the right to take a shortcut across your neighbour's garden so that you could get home more quickly. You might have a right to light – enabling the light coming through your window so that you can enjoy 'comfortable' use of your premises. You might have the right to park your car on someone else's land.

So you are beginning to realise that easements can quite often give rise to disputes and/or ill feeling between the dominant and the servient owners. It has even been held in one disputed case that someone had an easement which was the right to use another person's lavatory.

Some easements are blindingly obvious. If you live in a terraced house or a semi-detached property, mutual easements of support are pretty essential if you don't want both houses to collapse.

What can you do if you are entitled to an easement and the servient (see how useful these terms are to you after all?) owner impedes your use of it; for example, you are entitled to cross his or her field but one day you find that he or she has padlocked the gate through which you would gain access?

There is a remedy called 'abatement' – sorry, another legal term but easements bristle with them. Abatement, in the case of the impeded entry to the field, may take the form of your breaking the lock on the padlock. However, you need to be careful if you opt for this kind of remedy because the courts tend not to be particularly happy about your taking matters into your own hands, even if your action can be covered by a legal term.

Judges have a phrase of their own to describe what abatement means – it must be the 'least mischievous' method of putting the situation right; in other words, you must refrain from causing 'unnecessary' damage. Here you will be treading a fine line, since what seems necessary to you in the heat of the moment may not seem so to the judge.

You could take the alternative court route of seeking an injunction against the padlocker, or damages and/or a declaration of your right against your neighbour. On the whole, it may just be best to try to get on with him or her as well as you can, in the hope that no disagreements arise.

FIXTURES AND FITTINGS

When you buy a property, so the old common law held, you were buying the land, the buildings on it, the soil, the rocks beneath and the air above. Just imagine if you could still claim the air – all those jumbo jets would have to get your permission to fly over your garden. You could even charge the airlines for the privilege!

When you purchase a home today, anything fixed or permanently attached to it should also be yours. But you may have had the experience I had when I moved into my newly purchased home, only to discover that the light fittings had all been completely removed, leaving a couple of bare wires dismally poking through the ceilings in all the rooms. You may also have heard horror stories about unfortunate purchasers who have found all the bathroom fittings unscrewed, down to the toilet roll holder. Not much you can do about that, apart from wondering why people like that don't get themselves a life.

So it really is essential, if you are the buyer, to make sure of just what is and what isn't included in the sale. A detailed list should be agreed by both you and the vendor so that annoyance can be avoided on both sides.

Things growing on the land are normally regarded as part of the fixtures and fittings, but the seller may indicate that there are particularly prized shrubs or other plants which he or she does not wish to include in the sale. Fitted carpets can sometimes be a matter of dispute, so make sure that they are included if you want them. You might have to pay an additional sum, but it might be worth it. When it comes to the kitchen, you will want to know exactly what is included. Things like washing machines, dishwashers, refrigerators and freezers, for example, may not be.

As with other areas of the law, disagreements about what should be fixtures and fittings throw up some fascinating judicial decisions. A peer of the realm, Y, sold X his stately home. When X arrived to take possession of it he discovered that Y had taken a number of portraits which had been screwed to the walls. Not only that, he had removed an imposing statue of a Greek god which had been decorating the garden. X sued Y and the case got as far as the Court of Appeal.

You and I might think that X clearly had right on his side. But a majority of the court held that the pictures had not been an intrinsic part of the design of the room from which they had been removed. So far as the statue was concerned, it had stood on a plinth, which had been left by the vendor. The court decided that it was only the plinth which had been attached to the land; consequently, the removal of the Greek god wasn't wrongful.

So X was left with an empty plinth and a large legal bill. Be warned.

I CAN TELL MY HAIRDRESSER ANYTHING...

From time immemorial women have confided in their hairdressers. The soothing ambience of the salon, the intimate attention to your appearance being given by someone with a sympathetic ear, and the opportunity to relax during the various treatments all combine to encourage us to talk freely about our problems as to our dearest friends.

But there is a new danger in opening our hearts to those wielding the scissors or the hair colourants. It has been reported that some firms of solicitors, wishing to drum up custom for themselves, are offering payments in cash to hairdressers who will pass on to them the names of women who are experiencing difficulties in their marriages.

It is an ingenious method of building up a client list in the family law department. The two professionals most likely to be told about problems in the marital area are the general practitioner and the hairdresser.

Since GPs still have ethical rules about confidentiality to which they conform, no information is going to be passed on to solicitors from the surgery. Consequently, it is the hairdressers who have been targeted in this rather sleazy attempt to win clients. One solicitor who pays for such information explained, when interviewed, that a 'tactful' approach will be made to the dissatisfied wife who has been identified. She will be offered a free consultation lasting 30 minutes and will be given advice about seeking a decree – with his firm acting for her, of course.

I don't know whether solicitors still go in for ambulance chasing – when victims of accidents had business cards pressed upon them as they lay on stretchers, inviting them to sue whoever they thought to be responsible for their plight – but this new form of pressurised salesmanship runs that practice a pretty close second.

At one time lawyers were not permitted to advertise, but that restriction has been removed, as anyone who listens to commercial radio stations will be only too aware. Apparently, in the men's rooms in some City wine bars an enterprising firm advertises itself under the slogan, 'Ditch the bitch'. Having no personal acquaintance with men's rooms, I am unable to confirm this, but I am happy to report that we certainly don't come across anything similar in women's facilities.

Most wives get fed up with their spouses from time to time – that is an inevitable consequence of being married. But just imagine the horror of a wife who has blabbed a routine moan about some shortcoming exhibited by her husband, and who is 'tactfully' approached by divorce lawyers. And just imagine the scene should this tactful approach come to the notice of said husband!

Sensible hairdressers might like to put a printed disclaimer in their shop windows to the effect that no information communicated to personnel will be transmitted to solicitors. Otherwise, wary clients may vote with their feet.

AGE DISCRIMINATION IS A THING OF THE PAST

It certainly ought to be extinct in view of the legislation which came into force in October 2006.

Age-based prejudice has been described as the 'last bastion' of unlawful discrimination in the workplace. We needn't kid ourselves, however, that the idea of making it unlawful in the workplace stems solely from a milk of human kindness approach to senior citizens. They will still be discriminated against when it comes to keeping their pensions in line with the cost of living, for example.

No, the new encouragement for older people to keep on working is based on sheer economic necessity. We are increasingly a top-heavy population, with too few workers paying taxes which will support ever-increasing numbers of pensioners. It is a problem which cannot be ameliorated, since birth control and abortion will continue to limit the numbers of babies being born who could eventually replace those who retire.

So what does it all mean? Employers are no longer allowed to make decisions based on age. Employers cannot insist on dates of birth being supplied by job

applicants. And a good thing too. Hopefully, this will mean that other organisations will not be able to insist that you give details of your chronological age, in situations where there is no justification whatsoever for that insistence.

I have been conducting my personal age-resistant campaign for several years. If I consider the question on a form intrusive and unnecessary in the circumstances, I write 'over 21' in the box.

The set retirement age under the new legislation is 65, but this is to be reviewed in 2011, after five years. If the government takes the view that the economy no longer needs a default retirement age of 65, it will be abolished. The way things are going, with many older people living healthy and energetic lives into their 80s and birth rates continuing to fall short of the numbers needed, watch out for the possibility that, far from abolition, it may be increased to 70.

Insulting ageist comments made in the workplace, 'stupid old trout' or 'silly old git', for example, now entitle an employee to sue for unlawful discrimination, if the employer in question has not taken action to ensure that they are not made. But to look for legal compensation may turn out to be a two-edged sword, as it has done in other cases where sexual or racial discrimination has given rise to a complaint. The complainant can find that he or she has a reputation which will make it difficult or impossible to find other employment.

Will the new law result in a rush of tribunal applications by senior citizens? Impossible to say. Maybe the government should make it illegal to discriminate against anyone who has made an application to the employment tribunal!

POSSESSION IS NINE TENTHS OF THE LAW

When you come to think of it, why should it be? From those who drape towels over sunbeds round a resort swimming pool before other less determined holidaymakers have shaken the sleep from their eyes (not an exclusively German habit incidentally) to people who assure you that 'these seats are taken' when there isn't anywhere else to sit and none of the other presumed occupants put in an appearance, there are still some of us who like to adhere rigidly to the selfish principle embodied in this ancient adage.

Its origins probably spring from the old common law doctrine known as 'adverse possession'. In short, the principle became established that if A had managed to occupy land belonging to B for a period of 12 years, with no complaint from B, A would be entitled to ownership of that land.

It is not difficult to understand why this rule came into operation before the introduction of land registration in this country, at a time when occupation was the most obvious proof of ownership. Perhaps it is less understandable that it continued to operate even after the true owner could establish his or her right at the Land Registry.

Why B, as the owner of land occupied by A, would leave that occupancy undisturbed for as long as 12 years might be a mystery – you would think that was a rare occurrence. But it was more common than you would expect. Needless to say, the law surrounding the concept was extremely complex (far too complex to go into here), but cases were still being fought and won over adverse possession until the whole situation had to be re-examined as a result of a case taken to the European Court of Human Rights, under the Human Rights legislation now in force in this country.

In that case A was a farmer and had been farming land belonging to B for more than 12 years. He succeeded, on the ground of adverse possession, in defeating B's claim that the land should be returned to him. The case went as far as the House of Lords, our ultimate court of appeal.

However, thanks to the new law, B was able to take his case to Europe. The European Court of Human Rights disapproved of the principle that anyone could acquire entitlement to someone else's land simply by occupancy for a certain period. The court found that to deprive B of his ownership solely on the ground that A had occupied it for more than 12 years was a breach of B's human rights.

So it looks as though possession is no longer to be nine tenths of the law. Could this mean that now we'll all be able to pitch those towels into the swimming pool and park ourselves in those vacant seats with impunity?

HOW UNREASONABLE DO YOU HAVE TO BE?

Claiming that your husband or wife has behaved so unreasonably that you cannot be expected to put up with it is a popular route to a quick divorce. Of the five possible ways to prove that you are entitled to a divorce decree, the only other speedy method would be to prove that he or she has committed adultery. If, for some reason, this is impossible or inconvenient, the remaining options take up considerably more waiting time.

To proceed on desertion, you have to be deserted for a period of two years. Even for a civilised divorce by consent, where no allegation is made on either side, you still have to have lived apart for two years. If no other ground is open to you and your spouse refuses to consent to a decree, you have to wait five years. In today's climate, having to wait even two years is totally unacceptable to most would-be candidates for divorce. Consequently, unreasonable behaviour may be the preferred choice.

So, how unreasonable does your husband or wife's behaviour have to be? The truth is that any competent family lawyer can assemble sufficient ammunition to satisfy the court on this ground from the daily minutiae of any couple's relationship. The test, you see, is not really an objective one. What is unreasonable in the eyes of the law can be conduct which the petitioner – the person seeking the divorce – finds unreasonable, and that test can be highly subjective.

One man succeeded in proving that his wife had behaved unreasonably by giving evidence that she fed better meals to their cats than to him. One woman, married to a do-it-yourself enthusiast, got a divorce on the ground that he started jobs around the house and then left them unfinished for an unconscionable time – notably in the instance where he removed the door of the lavatory and failed to replace it for several months.

Lack of appreciation is a common matrimonial fault. Criticising your spouse in the presence of family or friends could prove to be a fruitful source of complaint. Frequently a wife will object to the hours her husband spends at work and away from the family. The mirror image of that will be the husband who moans that his wife expects him to work overtime to provide her with luxuries.

In days gone by, behaviour petitions frequently provoked furious respondents into filing answers – formal pleadings in response to the petitions – which denied everything. Some went further and issued cross-petitions making allegations of their own. This is still possible for those wealthy and indignant enough to fund the considerable expense. For most, wiser counsel will prevail. They will swallow their bile and allow the petition to take its course.